Contents

Double Chocolate Gelato 6

Canna Cherry-Strawberry Gelato 6

Peaches-N-Cream Soft Serve Ice Cream 7

Tropical Mango Soft Serve Ice Cream 7

Lime Coconut Ice Pops 8

Rose Coconut Ice Cream 8

Pumpkin Flan with Pumpkin Seed Praline 9

Lemon Panna Cotta 10

Tropical Coconut Pudding 11

Healthy Chia Seed Pudding 12

Canna Rice Pudding with Raisins and Apricots 12

Canna Banana Parfait 13

Get High Pudding 14

Marijuana Creamy Custard 15

"Baked" Peach Pie 15

Fresh Glazed Very Red Berry Pie 16

Blueberry-Peach Cobbler 17

Chocolate Citrus Torte 18

Lemon Raspberry Scones 18

Chocolate Coconut Pecan Pie 19

Stoned Gummies 20

Ganja Toffee Chews 21

Juanita's Canna Lollipop 21

Canna Mint Patties 22

Tropical Orange Chews 22

Peanut Butter Cups 23

Chocolate Covered Cherries 24

Canna Chocolate Truffles 24

Marijuana Fudge Munchies 25

Oat Munchies Spheres 25

Pavlov with Canna-Raspberry Sauce 26

Cannabis Easter Egg 27

Weed-Infused Sugar Cookie Christmas Tree 28

Cannabis-Infused Birthday Cake 29

Weed Donuts..30

Weed Macaroons...30

Weed Cotton Candy...32

Cannabis Coffee Cake..32

Weed Popsicles..33

For Medicated Coconut Oil 34

Cannabis Granola...34

Cannabis No-Bake Toffee Cookies 35

Cannabis Chocolate Birthday Cake..36

Cannabis Banana Muffins 36

Cannabis Coconut Creme Brûlée...37

Cannabis Tiramisu..38

Chocolate Ganache Cannabis Cupcakes..39

Chocolate Canna-Cups Recipe 39

Tricolor Marshmellow Cereal Treats 40

Cannabis Thumbprint Tea Cookies Recipe..41

No-Bake Fudge...41

Chocolate-Dipped Weed Cherries...42

Cannabutter Pound Cake...42

Cannabis Taffy..43

Cannabis Corn Syrup..43

Canna-Banana Bread..44

Red Velvet Canna Cake..44

Cherry- Cranberry Ginger Cake 45

Peach Jelly Roll...46

Silky Coconut Cake...47

Cannabis Strawberry Cake...48

Stoner's Lemon Poppy Seed Loaf..48

Choco-Espresso Spelt Cake..49

Canna Cinnamon Coffee Cake..50

Canna Apple Pecan Space Cake...51

Canna Carrot Muffins 52

Rum Raisin Cupcakes..52

Hot Ganja Chocolate Cupcakes..54

French Toast Cupcakes...54

Cannabis Hummingbird Cupcakes...55

Kirsch Chocolate Muffins..57

Canna- Banana Crumble Muffins...57

Cannabis Pancakes...58

Cannabis Carrot Cake..58

Marijuana Cheesecake...59

Cannabis Gingerbread...60

Chocolate Cannabis Bar..60

Cannabis Basic Muffins...61

Chewy Chocolate Chip Weed Cookies....................................61

Peanut Butter Bud Bars..62

Chronic Apple Crisp...63

Space Cake...63

Cannabis Sugar Cookies...64

Strawberry Weed Muffins..65

Adult Weed Brownies...65

Hot Canna Cocoa...66

Lemonade...67

Marijuana Milkshake..67

Thai Iced Tea...68

The Proper Pineapple Smoothie..68

Mayonnaise...69

Caesar Salad Dressing...70

Lemon Vinaigrette..70

BBQ Sauce..71

Pesto...72

Sriracha Hot Sauce...73

Guacamole..73

Spiced Nuts..74

Spicy Chickpeas...75

Savory Popcorn..76

Potato Chips..76

Buffalo Chex Mix...77

Baked Kale Chips...78

Hush Puppies...79

No-Bake Cannabis Cookie Bars...80

Chocolate Bananas..80

Creamy Stuffed Cannabis-Infused Pancakes................................81

Chocolate Weed Brownies..81

How to Make Weed Candy...82

Cannabis Caramel Candy...83

Caramel Cashew Squares...83

Homemade Cannabis Oreo Cookies...84

Cannabis Chocolate Ice Cream with Super Potent Blondies..............85

Cannabis Chocolate Caramel Peanut Butter Cups.........................86

Potent Cannabis Brownies...87

Cannabis-Infused Ice Cream...88

Weed Banana Bread...88

OMFG MINT CANNABIS BROWNIES...89

Poppy-Pot Cake..89

Purple Kush Cake..90

Canna Coffee and Tea...91

Iced Canna Coffee...91

Chocolate Olive Oil Cake...92

Orange Almond Cake..93

Chocolate-Covered Pretzels...93

S'mores Cannabis Brownies..94

Peanut Brittle..95

Marshmallows..96

Pop Tarts...97

Rice Krispie Treats..98

Candied Bacon...99

Chocolate Strawberries...100

Cheeba Chocolate Chip Cookies...101

Pumpkin Pot Brownies...102

Rocky Road Marijuana Brownies...102

Honey Chocolate Brownies...103

Microwave Peanut Butter Swirl Brownie..104

CannaCrack..104

Oven-Baked Donut Holes...105

Baked Backlava...106

Butterscotch Canna-Pops..106

INGREDIENTS:...106

Cannabis Hard Candy..107

INGREDIENTS:...107

Pina Co-Canna Pie Cake..108

Red-Hot White Fudge...108

Cannabis Hard Candy and Lollipop..109

Cannabis Toffee Candy...110

Cannabis Peanut Butter Balls..111

Rice Krispie Treats...111

Cannabis Apple Pie...112

Cannabis-Infused Red Velvet Cake...113

DOUBLE CHOCOLATE GELATO

Preparation Time: 15 -20 minutes- **Cooking Time:** 5 to 10 minutes - **Servings**: 4-6

INGREDIENTS:

- 1/2 cup heavy cream
- 2 cups of milk
- 3/4 cup sugar
- 1/4 teaspoon salt
- 7 ounces high-quality dark chocolate
- 1 teaspoon vanilla extract
- Cannabis butter

DIRECTIONS:

1. The first step is done by melting the chocolate, then cooling it for a bit. Place the milk, cream, and cannabis butter in a bowl and mix them together until well combined. Mix in the sugar by using a whisk and salt. Continue to whisk for about 4 minutes until the sugar and salt dissolve. Then mix in the vanilla extract. Finally, mix in the chocolate until well combined. Pour the ingredients into your ice cream maker, and let it churn for 25 minutes. Put the gelato in an airtight container and place in the freezer for up to 2 hours, until desired consistency is reached.

Nutrition:

Calories: 230, Fat: 9g, Fiber: g, Carbs: 60.1g, Protein: 4g

CANNA CHERRY-STRAWBERRY GELATO

Preparation Time: 20 minutes- **Cooking Time:** 0 minutes - **Servings**: 4-6

INGREDIENTS:

- 1/2 cup heavy cream
- 2 cups of milk
- 3/4 cup sugar
- Cannabis butter*
- 1 cup sliced strawberries
- 1 tablespoon vanilla extract

DIRECTIONS:

1. Using a blender, puree the strawberry thoroughly. Place the milk, cream, and cannabis butter in a bowl and mix them together until well combined. Mix in the sugar by using a whisk. Continue to whisk for

about 4 minutes until the sugar dissolves. Then mix in the vanilla extract and strawberry puree. Pour the ingredients into your ice cream maker, and let it churn for 25 minutes. Put the gelato in an airtight container and place in the freezer for up to 2 hours, until desired consistency is reached.

Nutrition:

Calories: 210, Fat: 6.8g, Fiber: 6g, Carbs: 34.6g, Protein: 3g

PEACHES-N-CREAM SOFT SERVE ICE CREAM

Preparation Time: 35 minutes- **Cooking Time:** 0 minutes - **Servings**: 4-6

INGREDIENTS:

- 2 cups heavy cream
- 1 cup milk
- 3⁄4 cup sugar
- Cannabis butter
- 1 Tbs. vanilla extract
- 1 cup sliced peaches

DIRECTIONS:

1. Using a blender, puree the peaches thoroughly. Place the milk, cream, and cannabis butter in a bowl and mix them together until well combined. Mix in the sugar by using a whisk. Continue to whisk for about 4 minutes until the sugar dissolves. Then mix in the vanilla extract. Then mix in the peaches. Put all the prepared ingredients in a clean ice cream maker and let it churn for 25 minutes. Serve immediately.

Nutrition:

Calories: 240, Fat: 6g, Fiber: 2g, Carbs: 56g, Protein: 1.5g

TROPICAL MANGO SOFT SERVE ICE CREAM

Preparation Time: 35 minutes- **Cooking Time:** 0 minutes - **Servings**: 6

INGREDIENTS:

- 2 cups heavy cream
- 1 cup milk
- 3⁄4 cup sugar
- 1 Tbs. vanilla extract

- 1 cup pureed mango (about 2.5 mangos)
- Juice of 1 lime
- Cannabis butter

DIRECTIONS:

1. Puree the mangos with the lime juice in a food processor or blender.
2. Place the milk, cream, and cannabis butter in a bowl and mix them together until well combined. Use a whisk to mix in the sugar. Continue to whisk for about 4 minutes until the sugar dissolves. Then mix in the vanilla extract. Then mix in the mango puree.
3. Put all the prepared ingredients in a clean ice cream maker and let it churn for 25 minutes.
4. Serve immediately.

Nutrition:

Calories: 176, Fat: 2.1g, Fiber: 6g, Carbs: 36g, Protein: 0.4g

LIME COCONUT ICE POPS

Preparation Time: 10 minutes- **Cooking Time:** 0 minutes - **Servings**: 4

INGREDIENTS:

- 1 14 ounces canna coconut milk, canned
- 1 cup cream
- 2 tablespoons limeade concentrate
- 1 tablespoon lime zest
- 2 tablespoons lemon juice
- Pinch of salt

DIRECTIONS:

1. Toss in all the ingredients in the blender. Puree until it forms a smooth mix. Transfer mix into Popsicle molds. Freeze molds.

Nutrition:

Calories: 180, Fat: 2.5g, Fiber: 8g, Carbs: 35.9g, Protein: 0.2g

ROSE COCONUT ICE CREAM

INGREDIENTS:

- ⅓ cup Rose Tea
- 2 ¾ cup canna cream
- 10 egg yolks
- 5 tablespoons Simple Syrup

- 1 cup coconut, shredded

DIRECTIONS:

1. In a double boiler heat until nearly boiling and remove from the heat rose tea and cream. In a separate bowl, whisk until frothy eggs and milk. Pour the warm milk over the eggs whisking continually, then back into the pan over low heat. Cook and stir until the mixture thickens.
2. The mixture must be strained to a clean bowl and add coconut. Cover with plastic wrap and cool at room temperature. Pour into an electric ice cream machine and follow the manufactures direction.

Nutrition:

Calories: 190, Fat: 3.2, Fiber: 3g, Carbs: 45g, Protein: 0.6g

PUMPKIN FLAN WITH PUMPKIN SEED PRALINE

Preparation Time: 6 hrs. (For cooling)- **Cooking Time:** 1-2 hrs. - **Servings**: 4-6

INGREDIENTS:

- 1¾ cups granulated sugar
- 1 cup whole milk
- 2 (5-ounce) cans evaporated milk
- 2 tablespoons plus
- 2 teaspoons canna sugar
- 5 large eggs
- ¼ teaspoon salt
- 1¾ cups pure pumpkin puree
- 2 tablespoons tequila
- 1 tablespoon orange zest
- 2 teaspoons ground cinnamon
- 1 teaspoon ground ginger
- ¼ teaspoon ground cardamom
- ¼ teaspoon freshly grated nutmeg
- 1 tablespoon pure vanilla extract
- Pumpkin Seed Praline
- Vegetable oil, for greasing the foil
- 1 cup granulated sugar
- Pinch of salt
- ½ cup of water

- 1 cup hulled (green) pumpkin seeds, toasted

DIRECTIONS:

1. Preheat the oven to 375°F. Set a 2-quartsoufflé dish or round ceramic casserole in the middle of the oven to preheat. Using a pot, bring water to a boil. In a dry, heavy, 2-quart saucepan, heat 1 cup of the granulated sugar over medium-low heat, stirring slowly with a fork until the sugar melts and turns golden brown. Cook, without stirring, swirling the pan, until the sugar is deep amber, about 5 minutes. This is your caramel. Remove the hot soufflé dish from the oven and immediately pour the caramel into the dish, tilting it to cover the bottom and sides completely. Set it aside to harden while you prepare the rest of the flan. (Leave the oven on.) Ina medium saucepan, combine the whole milk and the evaporated milk. Bring to a gentle simmer over medium heat, and then remove from the heat. Pour the milk mixture through a fine-mesh sieve into a bowl; set aside. Ina large bowl using an electric mixer, beat together the remaining¾ cup granulated sugar, the canna sugar, and the eggs on medium speed until smooth and creamy. Beat in the salt, pumpkin, tequila, orange zest, cinnamon, ginger, cardamom, nutmeg, and vanilla. While stirring, add the strained milk mixture in a slow stream and stir until it is mixed well Pour the custard over the caramel in the dish and set the dish in a roasting pan. Put in the boiling water in the pan until it comes about 1 inch up the sides of the soufflé dish. Put the pan in the middle of the oven and reduce the oven temperature to 350°F. Bake it until the color is golden brown on top and a knife inserted into the center of the flan comes out clean, 1¼ to 1½ hours. Take the baking dish out of the water bath and transfer it to a wire rack to cool. Refrigerate at least 6 hours. Prepare the praline: Preheat the oven to 250°F. Use an aluminum foil t line a baking sheet and lightly oil the foil. Set the baking sheet in the oven to keep warm. Ina deep, heavy, 2-quart saucepan, combine the sugar, salt, and ½ cup water and cook over medium-low heat, stirring slowly with a fork, until melted and pale golden. Cook the caramel without stirring, tilting the pan from side to side, until deep golden. Immediately stir in the pumpkin seeds and quickly pour the mixture onto the prepared baking sheet, spreading it into a thin sheet before it hardens. (when the caramel becomes too solid and is difficult to spread, raise the oven temperature to 400°F and place the baking sheet in the oven until the caramel is warm enough to spread, 1 to 2 minutes.) Let the praline cool on the baking sheet on a wire rack until completely hardened, and then break it into large pieces. To unmold the flan, run a thin knife around the edges to loosen it. Wiggle the dish from side to side; when the flan moves freely in the dish, invert a large serving platter with a lip over the dish. Holding the dish and platter securely together, quickly invert them together, turning the flan out onto the platter. The caramel will pool over and around it—this is exactly what you want to happen, so don't worry—it's normal. Slice the flan into wedges and serve with the caramel spooned over it, topped with shards of the praline.

Nutrition:

Calories: 289, Fat: 9g, Fiber: 2.5g, Carbs: 61g, Protein: 1.8g

LEMON PANNA COTTA

Preparation Time: 20 minutes plus a cooling time of 4 hrs.- **Cooking Time:** 15 minutes - **Servings**: 6

INGREDIENTS:

- 1 envelope of unflavored gelatin
- 2 cups of Marijuana Milk
- 2 tablespoons of heavy cream
- 1/2 cup of sugar
- 2 teaspoons of pure vanilla extract
- 21/4 cups of plain yogurt (preferably Greek-style)
- 2 teaspoons of freshly squeezed lemon juice

For the Fruit Topping:

- 1 cup of raspberries, red and golden
- 2 cups of mixed strawberries or blueberries
- 2 peaches, peeled, thinly sliced
- 2 teaspoons of canna sugar
- 1 ounce of Vodka
- 1 ounce of Campari
- 1 tablespoon of lemon zest

DIRECTIONS:

1. Sprinkle the entire package of gelatin over 2 tablespoons of heavy cream in a small bowl. Let it soften for about 5 minutes. Combine the Marijuana Milk, sugar and vanilla in a saucepan over low heat. Bring this mixture to a simmer for a couple of minutes then remove the saucepan from the heat. Stir the gelatin and cream mixture in a saucepan until it's all dissolved. Place the yogurt in a medium bowl and whisk until smooth. Gradually whisk the Marijuana Milk mixture and lemon juice into the yogurt. Pour mixture into six small ramekins. Cool it in the fridge for about 4 hours or until set. For the topping, toss the fruit, Vector Vodka, Cannabis Campari and sugar together with the lemon zest. Refrigerate for at least 20 minutes. To remove the Panna Cotta from the ramekins, run a sharp knife around the edges then invert the ramekin onto a plate. Top with fruit mixture and serve.

Nutrition:

Calories: 255, Fat: 6g, Fiber: 2.4g, Carbs: 50.1, Protein: 0.4g

TROPICAL COCONUT PUDDING

Preparation Time: 5 minutes- **Cooking Time:** 15 minutes - **Servings**: 2

INGREDIENTS:

- ¾ cup old-fashioned gluten-free oats
- ½ cup unsweetened shredded coconut

- 2 cups of water
- 1¼ cups coconut milk
- 2 teaspoons canna-oil (here)
- ½ teaspoon ground cinnamon
- 1 banana, sliced

DIRECTIONS:

1. Using a bowl, combine the oats, coconut, and water. Cover and chill overnight. Transfer the mixture to a small saucepan. Add the milk, canna-oil, and cinnamon, and simmer for about 12 minutes over medium heat. Remove from the heat, and let stand for 5 minutes. Divide between 2 bowls and top with the banana slices.
2. If you would prefer an even tastier treat, sauté the banana slices in a little butter and brown sugar before topping the pudding.

Nutrition:

Calories: 156, Fat: 1,3g, Fiber: 8.9g, Carbs: 49g, Protein: 2g

HEALTHY CHIA SEED PUDDING

Preparation Time: 35 minutes plus cooling time- **Cooking Time:** 0 minutes - **Servings**: 2

INGREDIENTS:

- 1½ cups almond milk
- 8 dates, pitted and chopped
- ⅓ cup chia seeds
- ¼ cup unsweetened cocoa powder
- 4 teaspoons canna-oil (here)
- ½ teaspoon ground cinnamon

DIRECTIONS:

1. Using a bowl, combine all the ingredients. Stir well. The next step is done by covering it with saran wrap and chill in the refrigerator overnight. Transfer the mixture to a blender and pulse several times until coarse and uniform. Pour the mixture into individual pudding bowls. Cover the remaining servings with plastic wrap and store in the refrigerator for up to a week.

Nutrition:

Calories: 160, Fat: 2g, Fiber: 8.8g, Carbs: 51g, Protein: 2.4g

CANNA RICE PUDDING WITH RAISINS AND APRICOTS

Preparation Time: 5 minutes- **Cooking Time:** 25 minutes - **Servings**: 6

INGREDIENTS:

- 3 cups whole milk
- 3 cups cooked white rice
- 2 tablespoons canna-butter (here)
- ½ cup raisins
- ½ cup chopped dried apricots
- ⅓ cup brown sugar
- ¼ teaspoon ground cinnamon
- 2 teaspoons vanilla extract

DIRECTIONS:

1. Using a medium saucepan, combine the milk, rice, canna-butter, raisins, apricots, sugar, and cinnamon. Bring to a boil, then immediately reduce the heat. Simmer gently over low heat for 25 minutes or until the rice is tender. Stir in the vanilla. Serve warm. Store the remaining servings in an airtight container in the refrigerator for up to a week. Reheat in the microwave on low heat for 2 minutes or until warm, or enjoy chilled.

Nutrition:

Calories: 251, Fat: 6.1g, Fiber: 2.8g, Carbs: 53.2, Protein: 0.9g

CANNA BANANA PARFAIT

Preparation Time: 30 minutes plus cooling- **Cooking Time:** 30 minutes - **Servings**: 6

INGREDIENTS:

- 6 large egg yolks
- ¾ cup granulated sugar
- ¼ cup plus 2 tablespoons cornstarch
- ¼ heaping teaspoon salt
- 3½ cups whole milk
- 1 tablespoon unsalted cannabutter
- 1 tablespoon vanilla extract
- 1 tablespoon spiced rum
- ½ cup cold heavy cream
- 2 tablespoons confectioners' sugar
- 2 cups broken shortbread cookies
- 3 large ripe bananas, sliced

DIRECTIONS:

1. Using a medium saucepan, stir together the egg yolks, granulated sugar, cornstarch, and salt over medium heat. Bring to a simmer and put in the milk while frequently stirring, 5 to 8 minutes. It starts bubbling, turns the heat down to low and continues cooking, constantly whisking, until the mixture thickens, which will take up to 2 minutes.
2. Put it away from the heat, and then add in the vanilla, canna-butter, and rum. Put the mixture to another bowl and place a piece of plastic wrap directly on the surface of the pudding to keep a film from forming. Refrigerate until set for a few hours.
3. Once the pudding is cold, place the cream in a bowl. Using a stand or electric mixer on medium-low speed, whip until the creamed well. Blend in the confectioners' sugar and whip until the cream holds silky, medium-firm peaks. Do not over mix
4. Into each of 6 parfait glasses, spoon a large dollop of the pudding mixture. Top with a layer of cookie pieces and a layer of sliced bananas. Do the same procedure and top it odd with the pudding. Crumble some of the cookie pieces and sprinkle over the top. Refrigerate until ready to serve.

Nutrition:

Calories: 215, Fat: 3g, Fiber: 1.4g, Carbs: 40.9, Protein: 0.9g

GET HIGH PUDDING

Preparation Time: 15 minutes- **Cooking Time:** 2 hrs. - **Servings**: 2

INGREDIENTS:

- 2cups dried figs soaked in 1/4 cup boiling water
- 1 cup of cannabis milk
- 1 1/2 cups all-purpose flour sifted
- 1 cup of sugar
- 2 1/2 teaspoons baking powder
- 1 tsp. pumpkin pie spice
- 1 teaspoon of sea salt
- 3 eggs
- 1/2 cup melted cannabis butter
- 1 1/2 cups breadcrumbs
- 1 tablespoon grated orange peel

DIRECTIONS:

1. Mix all ingredients until well blended. Pour into a greased bundt pan. Place into a water bath. Cover with nonstick foil loosely. Bake it until pudding is set and begins to release from the sides of the pan, about 2 hrs.

Nutrition:

Calories: 250, Fat: 4,7g, Fiber: 1.4g, Carbs: 49g, Protein: 0.9g

MARIJUANA CREAMY CUSTARD

Preparation Time: 15 minutes- **Cooking Time:** 15-20 minutes - **Servings**: 2

INGREDIENTS:

- 1 spoon vanilla extract
- 3 eggs
- 0.3 to 0.5 marijuana flowers
- 600 grams of milk
- 90-130 grams of sugar

DIRECTIONS:

1. In a medium-sized bowl, combine the eggs and milk Add vanilla extract, dried buds and sugar Beat everything at medium speed Once the liquid has formed, continue mixing the batter for an extra two minutes Transfer the contents into a container and then let it set in the fridge Dust with cinnamon or top with fruits.

Nutrition:

Calories: 208, Fat: 1.4, Fiber: 1.9g, Carbs: 35g, Protein: 0.2g

"BAKED" PEACH PIE

Preparation Time: 15-20 minutes- **Cooking Time:** 50-60 minutes - **Servings**: 6-8

INGREDIENTS:

- ½ cup plus 2 tablespoons canna sugar
- ¼ cup packed brown sugar
- 5 cups fresh peaches peeled and sliced (see Note)
- 1 prepared pie shell or Canna Pie Crust
- 3 tablespoons potato starch or cornstarch
- 1 teaspoon cinnamon, divided
- ½ teaspoon ground cloves
- ¼ teaspoons salt
- 1 tablespoon cannabutter
- 2 teaspoons lemon juice
- 3 tablespoons heavy cream

Canna Pie Crust:

- 3 cups all-purpose flour

- 14 tablespoons cold butter, cubed
- 2 tablespoons granulated sugar
- 2 tablespoons cannabutter, cold
- 1½ teaspoons salt
- ½ cup plus 2 teaspoons ice-cold water

DIRECTIONS:

1. Preheat the oven to 400°F. In a large bowl, combine ½ cup of the CBD sugar and the brown sugar, add the peaches, and toss to coat. Cover and let stand for 1 hour. Roll out half of the chilled pie dough and lay it in the bottom of a 9-inch pie pan. Trim the edges, leaving about ½ inch of crust overhang. Drain the peaches, reserving the juice. In a small saucepan, combine the potato starch, ½ teaspoon of the cinnamon, the cloves, and CBD salt, and slowly add in the reserved peach juice and stir. Put the pan over medium heat, and bring to a boil. Cook for 2 minutes or until thickened. Remove it from the heat and stir in the CBD butter and lemon juice. Pour the mixture over the peaches, carefully fold in, and then pour the filling into the crust. Roll out the remaining pastry and make a lattice or your favorite top crust. Trim, seal, and flute the edges. Mix together the remaining ½ teaspoon of cinnamon and 2 tablespoons CBD sugar. Brush the top of the uncooked pie crust with the cream and sprinkle with the cinnamon-sugar mixture. Cover the edges with foil, so they don't bake too quickly, and bake for 50 to 60 minutes, or until the filling is bubbly and the crust is golden.
2. Canna Pie Crust:
3. Mix together all the ingredients except water in the food processor. Pulse 4 to 5 times, then add the water, processing just until the dough comes together—you still want to see pea-size pieces of butter. Divide the dough into two equal pieces, wrap in plastic, and refrigerate for at least 1 hour or until ready to use.

Nutrition:

Calories: 289, Fat: 8.9g, Fiber: 2.8g, Carbs: 52.1, Protein: 0.9g

FRESH GLAZED VERY RED BERRY PIE

Preparation Time: 1 hr.- **Cooking Time:** 10-15 minutes - **Servings**: 3-4

INGREDIENTS:

- ½ cup regular sugar
- ½ cup canna sugar
- 1 pkg. Jell-O Raspberry Jelly Powder
- 2 tablespoon corn starch
- 1 cup of water
- 1 baked (9-inch) pie shell, cooled

- 3 cups fresh strawberries, hulled
- 2 cups fresh raspberries
- 1 cup heavy cream, whipped

DIRECTIONS:

1. Mix sugar, dry jelly powder and corn starch in a medium saucepan. Gradually Blend in water. Then let it boil under medium-high heat while whisking continuously. Cook and stir until thickened. Let cool 10 min. Fill pie shell with berries; cover with jelly glaze. Refrigerate 1 hour. Top with whipped cream before serving.

Nutrition:

Calories: 265, Fat: 5.4g, Fiber: 1.4g, Carbs: 67.1g, Protein: 1.2g

BLUEBERRY-PEACH COBBLER

Preparation Time: 20 minutes **- Cooking Time:** 45-50 minutes **- Servings**: 8

INGREDIENTS:

- ¼ cup (4 tablespoons/½ stick) unsalted butter, melted, plus more for the pan
- 4 cups sliced peeled peaches
- 1-pint blueberries (about 4 cups)
- 1 tablespoon cornstarch
- 1 teaspoon ground cinnamon
- ½ teaspoon ground ginger
- ¾ cup granulated sugar
- 2 tablespoons plus 2 teaspoons Canna sugar
- 1 cup all-purpose flour
- 2 teaspoons baking powder
- ⅛ teaspoon freshly grated nutmeg
- ⅛ teaspoon salt
- 1 cup whole milk Whipped cream, vanilla ice cream, or crème fraîche, for serving

DIRECTIONS:

1. Preheat the oven to 350°F. Lightly butter a 3-quart baking dish. In a bowl, mix together the melted butter, peaches, blueberries, cornstarch, cinnamon, ginger, and ¼ cup of the granulated sugar. Ina medium bowl, whisk together the remaining ½ cup granulated sugar, canna sugar, flour, baking powder, nutmeg, and salt. Slowly whisk in the milk. Pour the batter into the prepared baking dish and top with the fruit mixture. Next, bake it until it is golden in color the filling is bubbling and thick around the edges, maybe around 45 minutes, serve hot from the oven topped with whipped cream, vanilla ice cream, or crème fraîche. Cover and refrigerate any leftover cobbler for up to 4 days.

Nutrition:

Calories: 255, Fat: 6g, Fiber: 2.4g, Carbs: 50.1, Protein: 0.4g

CHOCOLATE CITRUS TORTE

Preparation Time: 15 minutes plus cooling time- **Cooking Time:** 10-15 minutes - **Servings:** 4-6

INGREDIENTS:

- 1 canna pie crust
- 8 ounces dark chocolate, chopped fine
- 6 tablespoons butter, unsalted, cut in a piece
- 1 Canna Spicy Jelly Spice Blend
- 2 tablespoons orange zest
- 2 tablespoons grapefruit zest
- ¼ cup boiling water
- 1 egg yolk
- Whipped Cream for topping

DIRECTIONS:

1. Over a double boiler, melt on low chocolate, butter, orange zest, grapefruit zest. Then, Whisk for 3 minutes in a double boiler over low heat. Strain out the egg yolk and mix well with chocolate. Pour into cooled crust and chill. Top with Whip Cream.

Nutrition:

Calories: 245, Fat: 4.1g, Fiber: 3.4g, Carbs: 49.1, Protein: 0.10g

LEMON RASPBERRY SCONES

Preparation Time: 35-40 minutes- **Cooking Time:** 15-20 minutes - **Servings:** 8-10

INGREDIENTS:

- Scones
- 2-3 cups cake flour
- 2 tsp. baking powder
- 1/4 cup sugar
- 1/2 teaspoon ground cardamom
- 1 tablespoon lemon zest (zest of 1 lemon)
- 5 tablespoons cold canna-butter, cut into chunks
- 1 cup heavy cream, plus more for brushing before baking
- 1 cup frozen raspberry

- 1/2 teaspoon salt
- Glaze
- 1/3 cup lemon juice
- 2 1/2 cups confectioners' sugar
- 2 tablespoons heavy cream

DIRECTIONS:

1. Bring the temperature of your oven to 400 F. with a piece of parchment paper, line a baking sheet

2. Place salt, flour, sugar, baking powder, cardamom, and lemon zest in the bowl of a food processor and pulse one or two times to mix. Add cold cannabis-infused butter and pulse a few times until the mixture forms coarse crumbs. Blend in the cream and pulse a few times just until incorporated. Remove dough from food processor and place in a large bowl. Fold in berries. Gather dough into a disc, wrap in plastic wrap, and refrigerate for at least 30 minutes. To cut in butter and dry ingredients using a dough scraper, then mix in cream by hand before folding in berries.

3. Roll dough to about 1/2-inch thickness on a lightly floured surface. Use a three 1/2-inch round cutter to cut out circles. Place on the prepared baking sheet. The scones must be brushed with butter or cream and bake for about 15 minutes or until tops are lightly browned. Let cool completely before applying the glaze.

4. Prepare glaze by mixing lemon juice, confectioners' sugar and heavy cream until smooth. Pour glaze over cooled scones.

5. Freezer Friendly!
   Wrap fresh baked glazed scones individually in plastic wrap, place in a plastic freezer bag, and freeze. Bring to room temperature and enjoy.

Nutrition:

Calories: 241, Fat: 2.9g, Fiber: 4g, Carbs: 56g, Protein: 0.81g

CHOCOLATE COCONUT PECAN PIE

Preparation Time: 15-20 minutes- **Cooking Time:** 30 minutes - **Servings:** 8-10

INGREDIENTS:

- ¼ cup melted cannabutter
- ¾ cup of sugar
- 2¼ teaspoons vanilla extract
- 3 eggs slightly beaten
- 3 tablespoons all-purpose flour
- 6 ounces sweetened dark
- chocolate bar, finely chopped

- ½ cup chopped pecans
- ½ cup shredded unsweetened
- coconut
- 9-inch prepared piecrust
- Whipped cream for topping

DIRECTIONS:

1. Preheat your oven to 350°.In a bowl, put in sugar, melted cannabutter, and vanilla extract. Mix it well, and then add in the flour and the eggs gradually...Ensure it is combined thoroughly. Fold in the pecan nuts, chocolate and coconut. Next, pour the mixture into the prepared piecrust and bake for around 30 minutes. The pie will rise during baking. After baking, let it cool in a rack, and when done, serve it with whipped cream on top.

Nutrition:

Calories: 221, Fat: 5.6g, Fiber: 1.4g, Carbs: 41.7, Protein: 0.76g

STONED GUMMIES

Preparation Time: 15-20 minutes- **Cooking Time:** 5 minutes - **Servings**: 30 pcs

INGREDIENTS:

- Nonstick cooking spray
- 1 large packet (6 ounces) Jell-O, your preferred flavor
- Four ¼-ounce envelopes unflavored gelatin
- ½ cup of cold water
- ¼ cup Cannabis Tincture
- Cornstarch, for dusting
- Special equipment: silicone gummy molds, funnel or dropper

DIRECTIONS:

1. Grease the molds lightly with the cooking spray, then wipe with a paper towel, so very little oil remains. Place the molds on a rimmed baking sheet. In a small saucepan, whisk the Jell-O and gelatin together, then add the cold water and whisk to combine. Over medium heat, bring Jell-O mixture to a boil, then reduce heat to low and cook for 5 minutes, stirring often. Remove it from heat and let cool slightly. Add the tincture and mix well. Using a funnel or dropper, fill the molds. Place the baking sheet in the fridge and let chill for 15 minutes. Pop the gummies out of the molds and dust lightly with cornstarch to prevent sticking. Prolong its shelf life by Storing them in a glass container in the fridge.

Nutrition:

Calories: 128, Fat: 2.7g, Fiber: 1g, Carbs: 29.9g, Protein: 0.4g

GANJA TOFFEE CHEWS

Preparation Time: 15- minutes- **Cooking Time:** 15 minutes - **Servings**: 24, pcs.

INGREDIENTS:

- 2 packs of saltine crackers
- 8 ounces of cannabutter
- 1 cup dark brown sugar
- 2 cups some flavor of confection chips semi-sweet, raspberry chocolate etc.
- 3/4 cup chopped nuts of your choice, depending on your flavor of chips.

DIRECTIONS:

1. First, line a half-size baking pan with 1 inch's sides with foil. Use a cooking spray to grease the foil and evenly distribute it, in a single layer, the saltine crackers, so they are covering the bottom of the pan but not overlapping. Also, preheat the oven to 350° and make sure the rack is in the center position. Into a heavy-bottomed saucepan, add the medicated butter and the sugar. When the mixture is already boiling, time it for exactly 3 minutes and then remove from the heat.

2. Quickly pour the molten mixture over the saltines and spread to cover crackers completely. Bake in the oven for 10 minutes. Remove the pan from the oven and expect that during the baking process, the mixture bubbled and probably put the crackers in wonky positions, but that's okay. Just poke them around with a fork to realign them. When they straighten out, pour the morsels over the candy and let it rest for a few minutes while it melts. Spread the melted morsels over the entire pan and top with chopped nuts. Let cool, or if you are in a hurry, stick them in the freezer for a while! I keep individual medicated pieces wrapped and frozen. They are excellent on ice cream or alone.

Nutrition:

Calories: 134, Fat: 2.1g, Fiber: 3g, Carbs: 47.6g, Protein: 0.7g

JUANITA'S CANNA LOLLIPOP

Preparation Time: 5 minutes- **Cooking Time:** 20 minutes - **Servings**: 2

INGREDIENTS:

- 1 tbsp. cannabis tincture
- 1 cup of sugar
- 1/2 cup light corn syrup
- 1/4 cup of water
- 1 teaspoon of lemon extract or other flavors

DIRECTIONS:

1. In a medium saucepan, add sugar, light corn syrup, 1/4 cup of water. Slowly heat your pan until you

reach 300F while beating the whole process. Remove from the fire. Add your extract and cannabis tincture. Beat well so that your tincture is distributed in the mixture. Set up your lollipop shape and lollipop sticks. Pour the blend prepared molds and allow them to cool.

Nutrition:

Calories: 125, Fat: 2.1g, Fiber: 1g, Carbs: 29.4g, Protein: 0.2g

CANNA MINT PATTIES

Preparation Time: 15 minutes to 4 hrs. for cooling- **Cooking Time:** 0 minutes - **Servings**: 24 pcs

INGREDIENTS:

- ½ cup of light corn syrup
- 2 teaspoon of peppermint extract
- ½ cup of softened cannabutter
- 2 drops of food coloring (optional)
- 9 cups of sifted powdered sugar (about 2 pounds)

DIRECTIONS:

1. Use a mixing bowl to mix the corn syrup, peppermint extract, and slightly melted Baked Butter or margarine. Then add the sugar, a little bit at a time, and incorporate it into the mix. Add the amount of food coloring to achieve your desired color and blend well.
2. Roll this mixture into small balls. Place them a few inches apart from each other on a baking sheet that has been lined with wax paper. Use a fork to make each one flat.
3. Let the mint patties set in the refrigerator for several hours. Remove the patties from the refrigerator and let stand at room temperature for several days to dry out. After a few days, when the patties are dried out, transfer them to a container with an airtight lid and store them in the refrigerator. You'll make about 24 patties. Eat 3 to 4 patties per (regular size) person to get baked.

Nutrition:

Calories: 140, Fat: 2.g, Fiber: 1.7g, Carbs: 41g, Protein: 0.9g

TROPICAL ORANGE CHEWS

Preparation Time: 20 minutes- **Cooking Time:** 25-30 minutes - **Servings**: 24 pcs

INGREDIENTS:

- ½ cup of cannabutter
- 2 cups of brown sugar
- 2 slightly beaten eggs
- 2 teaspoons of vanilla

- 3 teaspoons of freshly grated orange rind
- 1 cup of flour
- 1 teaspoon of salt
- 2 teaspoons of baking powder
- 2 cups of shredded coconut
- 2 cups of chopped dates

DIRECTIONS:

1. Preheat oven to 350° F. Grease a 9 by 9-inch pan.
2. In a saucepan, melt the Baked Butter or margarine then remove the saucepan from the heat. Stir in the brown sugar, vanilla, and orange rind. Once those ingredients are well combined, add the eggs. In a bowl or on a piece of waxed paper, combine the dry ingredients. Make sure to sift the dry ingredient at least three times. Mix the wet and dry ingredients together until completely mixed. Pour the batter into a prepared baking dish. Bake for 25 to 30 minutes. Cut into 16 squares when thoroughly cooled. If you like, roll each square into a ball and roll in more coconut. One to one and a half pieces/squares/balls will get you baked.

Nutrition:

Calories: 130, Fat: 2.7g, Fiber: 1g, Carbs: 31g, Protein: 0.3g

PEANUT BUTTER CUPS

Preparation Time: 1 hr. or overnight- **Cooking Time:** 0 minutes - **Servings**: 24 cups

INGREDIENTS:

- 1 cup unsalted toasted almonds
- 1 cup pitted dates
- 2 tablespoons cocoa powder
- 1 tablespoon cannabutter
- ½ cup peanut or cashew butter
- 1 tablespoon almond flour
- 1 cup semisweet chocolate chips, melted
- 2 tablespoons canna oil
- ½ teaspoon almond extract
- 1 teaspoon vanilla extract
- Sparkling sugar, for finishing

DIRECTIONS:

1. Prepare your muffin tray by putting liners on it. By the utilization of a blender or food processor, blend together dates, almonds cocoa powder, and CBD butter and pulse until it holds together. Press about 1

tablespoon of the almond mixture into the bottom of each cupcake liner. In a small bowl, combine the peanut butter and almond flour. Spread about 1 teaspoon of the peanut butter mixture on top of each cup. Put the tray in the chiller until the peanut mixture is firm. Meanwhile, in a small bowl, mix the chocolate chips, oil, and extracts. Remove the tin from the freezer and carefully spoon about 1½ teaspoons of the chocolate over each cup and smooth to the edges. Sprinkle with the sparkling sugar, freeze until firm, and enjoy.

Nutrition:

Calories: 135, Fat: 2.5g, Fiber: 1.4g, Carbs: 31.5g, Protein: 0.3g

CHOCOLATE COVERED CHERRIES

Preparation Time: 1 ½ hr.- **Cooking Time:** 5 minutes - **Servings**: 12

INGREDIENTS:

- 24 cherries with stems (remove the pits or use dried ones)
- 1 cup milk chocolate chips
- 1 cup dark chocolate chips
- ¼ cup of cannabis coconut oil

DIRECTIONS:

1. In a microwave-safe bowl, heat dark chocolate chips, milk chocolate chips and cannabis coconut oil. Heat the mix for 20-seconds intervals and stir by turns until it has finally melted. Ensure the chocolate is not too hot. Cover the cherries with chocolate, and let the excess chocolate drip. Set the cherries onto a wax-lined paper. Once all the cherries are done, transfer them into the refrigerator for 1-hour Double coat the cherries if you want (transfer into the refrigerator again) Enjoy!

Nutrition:

Calories: 210, Fat: 4g, Fiber: 2.1g, Carbs: 35g, Protein: 0.8g

CANNA CHOCOLATE TRUFFLES

Preparation Time: 15-20 minutes- **Cooking Time:** 0 minutes - **Servings**: 10-12

INGREDIENTS:

- ½ cup cannabutter softened
- ½cup powdered sugar
- ¼cup unsweetened cocoa powder
- ½cup almond flour
- Large pinch salt
- Dash almond extract

- Dash vanilla extract
- 24whole almonds, toasted in cannabutter and Salt
- 1cup unsweetened shredded coconut

DIRECTIONS:

1. Line a baking sheet with parchment paper. In a bowl, put all the prepared ingredients except the whole almonds and coconut and mix gently until the mixture is fairly smooth. Roll teaspoons of the mixture between your palms into balls. (Work quickly, as the butter gets very soft quickly. Refrigerate for a few minutes if the mixture gets too soft.) If using the toasted almonds, tuck one into the center of each and roll again quickly to smooth things over. Place the coconut in a bowl and roll the balls in the coconut until coated. Place on the baking sheet and refrigerate to firm up. Store the munchies in a glass container in the fridge.

Nutrition:

Calories: 141, Fat: 2.1g, Fiber: 1.4g, Carbs: 31.5g, Protein: 0.2g

MARIJUANA FUDGE MUNCHIES

Preparation Time: 10 minutes- **Cooking Time:** 0 minutes - **Servings**: 6-8

INGREDIENTS:

- 1/2 Cup cannabutter
- 1/2 Cup Almond Butter
- 1/8 to 1/4 cup Honey
- 1/2 of a Banana, Mashed
- 1 tsp. Vanilla Extract
- any kind of nut butter
- 1/8 Cup Dried Fruit
- 1/8 Cup Chocolate Chips

DIRECTIONS:

1. In a blender or food processer, add in all the ingredients. Blend for several minutes until smooth.
2. Pour the batter into a loaf pan with the lining of baking paper. For larger chunks, use a mini loaf pan or double the recipe. Refrigerate or freeze until firm. Cut into 8 equal squares.

Nutrition:

Calories: 210, Fat: 2.9g, Fiber: 1.7g, Carbs: 31.9g, Protein: 0.4g

OAT MUNCHIES SPHERES

Preparation Time: 20 minutes- **Cooking Time:** 5 minutes - **Servings**: 6-8

INGREDIENTS:

- 3 cups of rolled oats
- 2 tablespoons of cocoa powder
- 1 ½ cups of cannabis-infused butter
- 3 tablespoons of honey
- ¼ cup of peanut butter

DIRECTIONS:

1. Place a saucepan over heat and add cannabis-infused butter to melt. Add all other ingredients to the pan; stir and cook for 5 minutes. Pour the mixture in a baking pan and refrigerate for 15 minutes. Roll the mixture into small balls and refrigerate again. Serve.

Nutrition:

Calories: 125, Fat: 1.2g, Fiber: 5g, Carbs: 38g, Protein: 1g

PAVLOV WITH CANNA-RASPBERRY SAUCE

Preparation Time: 20 minutes- **Cooking Time:** 30 minutes - **Servings**: 6

INGREDIENTS:

FOR THE MERINGUES

- 3 large egg whites, at room temperature
- ½ teaspoon cream of tartar
- Pinch salt
- ⅔ cup granulated sugar
- 2 teaspoons cornstarch
- 1 teaspoon white vinegar
- 1 teaspoon vanilla extract

FOR THE RASPBERRY SAUCE

- ½ cup of orange juice
- 2 teaspoons cornstarch
- pound raspberries, rinsed
- ¼ cup honey
- 1 tablespoon Canna-Coconut Oil
- Pinch salt

DIRECTIONS:

1. Preheat the oven to 275°F. Line a baking sheet with parchment paper. For the meringues, in a tall, metal

bowl, using an electric mixer on high speed, whip the egg whites, cream of tartar, and salt together until soft peaks form, about a minute. As you are running the mixer, gradually add the sugar, 2 tablespoons at a time. Continue to beat on high speed until stiff peaks form. If you feel the meringue between your fingers, it should be smooth. If you still feel the sugar granules, keep beating on medium speed until the sugar has fully dissolved. Add in the cornstarch, vinegar, and vanilla and whisk to incorporate. Spoon about ½ cup of the egg white mixture for each pavlova onto the prepared baking sheet. Using a spoon, spread each into a 3-inch concave circle, with higher sides and a slight hollow in the middle. You should have enough for 6 pavlovas.

2. Bake until very light tan in color, and the meringue seems set, 25 to 30 minutes. Turn off the oven, open the door a smidge, and allow the pavlovas to cool completely. For the raspberry sauce, in a small bowl, combine the orange juice and cornstarch. Stir to until smooth. Over low heat, in a small saucepan, combine the raspberries, honey, and canna-oil and mix well, mashing the raspberries into a smooth sauce as they soften. Add the cornstarch mixture, increase the heat to medium, and stir until the mixture begins to thicken, 4 to 5 minutes; the sauce will continue to thicken as it cools. Stir in the salt. Put it away from the heat and pour into a small pitcher. Top the pavlovas with equal portions of the raspberry sauce immediately before serving.

3. Storage: You can prepare the pavlovas hours in advance and store them in an airtight container at room temperature until ready to serve. The sauce can also be made in advance and stored in the refrigerator, covered. If the consistency is too thick and hard to pour, heat it in the microwave for 10 seconds or so. Once sauced, you need to eat the pavlovas immediately.

Nutrition:

Calories: 215, Fat: 2.7g, Fiber: 1.7g, Carbs: 53g, Protein: 1.2g

CANNABIS EASTER EGG

INGREDIENTS:

- 1/4 cup cannabis butter
- 1 cup chocolate (70% cocoa solids) or milk chocolate.

DIRECTIONS:

1. In a large bowl, mix your chocolate and cannabis butter.

2. Half-fill a small pan with water and bring to a gentle simmer over a low heat. Rest your bowl with chocolate on top, then allow to melt, stirring occasionally.

3. Using oven gloves, remove the bowl from the heat and leave to cool to 95 degrees F (35 °C). Check the temperature with a cooking thermometer.

4. Spoon the chocolate into your mold, one tablespoon at a time, tilting the mold so the chocolate covers the surface. Don't worry if you make a mess! Tip any excess chocolate back into the bowl.

5. Allow the chocolate to cool slightly, then, using a butter knife, scrape around the rim of the mold to get a clean edge.

6. Meanwhile, repeat steps 4 to 6 with the second mold.

7. Lay out some greaseproof paper and place the mold flat-side-down on top for 15 minutes or until the chocolate has completely set.

8. To remove your eggs from their molds, squeeze the casing gently, working your way around the edge (the warmth from your hands will help).

9. Brush the remaining melted chocolate around the rim of each of the chocolate egg halves, then gently press them together so they stick in place. Leave for a few minutes until the chocolate sets, then it's ready!

WEED-INFUSED SUGAR COOKIE CHRISTMAS TREE

INGREDIENTS:

- 3/4 cup unsalted butter, room temperature
- 1/4 cup cannabis butter, room temperature
- 1 cup sugar
- 1 large egg, room temperature
- 1 teaspoon pure vanilla extrac t
- 1/2 teaspoon almond extract
- 2 teaspoon baking powder
- 2 1/2 cups all-purpose flour
- 1/2 cup cocoa powder

For Buttercream:

- 1/2 cup unsalted butter, room temperature
- 1/4 cup cannabis sugar
- 1 teaspoon vanilla extract
- 1/2 teaspoon pure almond extract
- 3 cups confectioners' sugar, sifted
- 1 -2 tablespoons whole milk, you can use more if needed
- Green food color
- Pinch salt

DIRECTIONS:

For Cookies:

1. Preheat oven to 350 degrees F.

2. Add both butters to the bowl of your stand mixer and cream on medium-high for 1-2 minutes, or until butter is smooth.

3. With the mixer on low, slowly add the sugar and then the egg.

4. Scrape the bowl with the mixer off.

5. Turn mixer back on low and add in extracts.

6. Allow all ingredients to combine fully .

7. Add the baking powder and then the flour, 1/2 cup at a time, until fully incorporated; ending with the cocoa powder.

8. Remove bowl from mixer and drop dough onto a floured countertop. Roll out into a flat disc, about 1/2 inch thick.

9. Cut cookies into 2-inch, 1 1/2-inch, and 1-inch cookies and bake for 6-9 minutes.

 Let cool on the cookie sheet until firm enough to transfer to a cooling rack.

For Buttercream:

1. Beat butter together with cannabis sugar in the bowl of stand mixer with paddle attachment on medium-high speed until light and fluffy (about 3 minutes).

2. With the mixer off or on low, add vanilla and almond extract.

3. Slowly add in confectioners' sugar, cannabis sugar, milk, green food color and salt; frequently scrape sides and bottom of the bowl.

4. Once incorporated, whip frosting for at least 3 minutes on medium-high to high.

5. If frosting is too thick to spread, gradually beat in additional milk.

6. Store in refrigerator up to 2 weeks. Rewhip before using.

CANNABIS-INFUSED BIRTHDAY CAKE

INGREDIENTS:

- 1/2 cup cannabis butter
- 1 cup butter
- 1 cup flour
- 1/2 teaspoon baking powder
- 6 eggs
- 1 cup sugar
- 1 teaspoon vanilla extract
- 3 cups powdered sugar
- 8 ounces cream cheese food coloring (optional)
- Jam (optional)

DIRECTIONS:

1. Preheat oven to 220 degrees F .

2. In a large bowl, blend 6 eggs with 1 cup sugar and vanilla extract until you get a nice white creamy mixture.

3. Fold in 1 cup flour and baking powder.

4. Pour into a cake pan and bake for 50 minutes.

5. In a medium bowl, cream together 1 cup butter with 1/2 cup cannabis butter.

6. Add powderd sugar, cream cheese and food coloring (optional).

7. Once cake is done, cool down and start glazing the cake with the cream mixture.

8. Decorate as you like and put in some candles.

WEED DONUTS

INGREDIENTS:

- 1 1/2 cups cannabis sugar
- 3/4 cup lukewarm milk
- 1 envelope yeast
- 1 tablespoon sugar
- 1 egg
- 1/4 cup melted butter
- 1/3 cup sugar
- 2 1/2 cups flour
- 1/2 teaspoon salt

DIRECTIONS:

1. In a medium bowl, add milk, 1 tablespoon sugar and yeast. Whisk and set aside .

2. In another bowl, add 1 egg, 1/3 cup sugar, melted butter and whisk.

3. Add yeast mixture to the egg mixture and whisk well.

4. In a large bowl, add flour, salt and wet mixture; mix and knead until smooth and no longer sticky.

5. Move the dough to a greased bowl and cover; set aside until it has doubled in size.

6. When doubled in size, knead dough once more and flatten out on a surface using a bread roller.

7. Cut donut-sized rounds in the dough using a round cutter.

8. Place on a flat tray and let double in size again.

9. Now fry your donuts for 2 minutes each side in vegetable oil on 350 degrees F.

10. Coat with cannabis sugar straight after frying.

11. Fill donuts with jelly or nutella.

WEED MACAROONS

INGREDIENTS:

- 1 1/3 cups of flaked coconut
- 1/3 cup of sugar
- 2 tablespoons flour
- Pinch of salt
- Egg whites of 2 eggs
- Vanilla extract
- 2 tablespoons of cannabis butte r
- Baking chocolate or chocolate chips
- Chopped nuts (optional)

DIRECTIONS:

1. Preheat oven to 325 degrees F and grease a large biscuit sheet or tray.

2. Combine together in a bowl the coconut, sugar, flour and salt. Use your hands to mix them well and break off any large lumps of coconut or flour. Once they are mixed well, set them aside and move on to the egg whites.

3. Crack the eggs and separate the egg whites from the yolks into a bowl. Then add half a teaspoon of vanilla extract to the egg whites.

4. Whip the egg whites very fast with a whisk or an electric hand mixer to get a nice, shiny and frothy mixture. It is important to do this step well; otherwise, the egg whites will run out of the meringue while it's cooking.

5. Add the whisked egg whites and vanilla extract mixture to the dry coconut and flour mix and combine the dry and wet ingredients together by tossing them with wooden spoons as it gives them a light and fluffy look.

6. Once the mixture is ready, put one tablespoon scoops of the mixture on the greased biscuit tray. You will get about a dozen scoops from this mixture .

7. Put the tray into the preheated oven for 15 to 18 minutes until the macaroons are golden brown. Keep an eye on them so they don't burn on the bottom.

For the Marijuana Chocolate:

1. For this you will need to prepare a double boiler with a pan filled with water and a glass bowl placed above it. Bring the water to a boil and then add the cannabis butter to the bowl and let it melt.

2. Once the butter has melted, start adding the chocolate to the cannabis butter in the bowl. As it melts, incorporate it gently with the butter using a spatula to get a glossy mixture. You can use any chocolate of your choice – milk, dark or white chocolate.

3. Check on the macaroons; they should be done by now. Take them out of the oven and let them cool for a few minutes before transferring them to a cooling wire rack.

4. Meanwhile, the chocolate sauce should be ready. Keep the flame on simmer so the sauce remains liquid. Once the macaroons have cooled down they are ready to be dipped in the marijuana chocolate sauce. Hold them from the bottom and dip the tops gently into the sauce. If you want the macaroons to be stronger you can double dip them in the marijuana chocolate again **5.** You can top them off with chopped nuts of your choice and voila! They are ready to be eaten.

WEED COTTON CANDY

INGREDIENTS:

- 2-3 weed candies
- 2 scoops flossine

DIRECTIONS:

1. Crush 2-3 weed candies using the mortar and pestle. Add flossine to the powder and crush it again. It's important to ensure that the powdered candy is smooth and fine.

2. Next, the powdered mixture needs to be spun into candy with the help of the cotton candy machine. To use the candy machine correctly, it's important to set it on a steady, flat and smooth surface. Also, ensure that the machine is placed at a safe height, away from the reach of children and pets. Once the necessary precautions are taken, the cotton candy machine is set to be used.

3. Once in place, turn on the candy machine's mortar and fill the floss head with about 2 scoops of the candy-flossine mixture. You might want to make sure that you are not filling more than 90% of the floss head.

4. The secret to spinning the perfect cotton candy is getting the details right, starting from the very beginning until the very last step.

5. After about 30-40 seconds of turning on the heat, you will see threads of the candy forming in the machine. Dip a lollipop stick inside and gather the cotton candy by twirling the stick around. Do not rotate the stick itself, but move it in a circular motion instead. Avoid touching the edges and turn off the machine once the cotton candy is done.

6. After a couple of trials, you'll be able to spin the perfect weed cotton candy, much to the amazement of those around you!

CANNABIS COFFEE CAKE

INGREDIENTS:

- 2 ¼ cups flour
- 1 package active yeast
- 2/3 cup milk
- 6 tablespoons vegetable shortening
- 6 tablespoons sugar

- 1/4 teaspoon salt
- 1 egg
- 1/2 cup sliced almonds
- 1 ½ tablespoons cannabis butter (melted)

DIRECTIONS:

1. Preheat oven to 375 degrees F.

2. In a medium mixing bowl, add I cup flour and the package of active yeast. Set it aside.

3. In a medium saucepan, add the milk, vegetable shortening and 4 tablespoons of sugar. Heat the pan and stir occasionally. Once the vegetable shortening has softened, remove the mixture from the heat and add the contents to the yeast and flour mixture.

4. Add the egg and beat ingredients for one minute in an electric mixture. Remove mixture from the sides of the bowl by scraping it and continue to beat the mixture for another 3 to 5 minutes. Slowly stir in the rest of the flour to form pliant dough.

5. Use the nonstick cooking spray to grease the baking pan. If you do not have cooking spray, grease it conventionally. Place the cake mixture into the baking pan. Sprinkle the top of the dough with sliced almonds and the remaining sugar. Cover it with a clean and damp dish cloth, and set aside for one hour to allow the dough to rise. Will normally take an hour or so.

6. Remove the dish cloth and drizzle the risen dough with melted cannabis butter. Bake for 17 to 20 minutes. Allow to cool. Slice, eat and feel heavenly.

WEED POPSICLES

INGREDIENTS:

- 2 mangos, peeled and in chunks
- 2 cups of your favorite vanilla yogurt
- 4 tablespoons cream of coconut
- 2-3 tablespoons of medicated coconut oil
- 3 tablespoons coconut sugar
- 2 teaspoons coconut extract
- If you do not like the taste of coconut, then you are more than welcome to use any substitute .

DIRECTIONS:

1. There are actually only four easy steps you need to follow to get yourself on your way to enjoying your popsicles, and those are as follows :

2. Place all of your ingredients into your blender.

3. Puree them until they are smooth.

4. Pour them into popsicle molds.

5. Freeze them.

6. And you are done! Once you are sure that your popsicles are nice and frozen, you can take them out of their mold and enjoy them! There has never been a simpler way to create an awesome medicated treat that you can enjoy on a hot summer day.

FOR MEDICATED COCONUT OIL

INGREDIENTS:

- 2 cups of coconut oil
- 1 ounce of medical marijuana

DIRECTIONS:

1. Making some medicated coconut oil for you to cook with is easy! All you have to do is place some coconut oil and cannabis in a pan, and simmer for 20 or so minutes. Once you are done, separate the leftover plant matter from the oil with a strainer. Make sure to get every last drop out of the plant matter so you do not waste anything.

2. Keep the heat low so that you do not mess with the THC levels of your cannabis. There have been a few studies that show that boiling cannabis can eliminate a lot of the THC which can ruin it for cooking or anything else. So, it is best to keep an eye on your cannabis while it is simmering.

3. Overall, this is a very simple recipe that you and any of your friends will love. As stated before, it is a completely customizable recipe, so you can change out any of the ingredients for something else. The possibilities are endless!

4. So go and create your weed popsicle today, and see what amazing frozen treat you make!

CANNABIS GRANOLA

INGREDIENTS:

- ½ cup of marijuana-infused coconut oil
- 3 cups of oatmeal
- 1 cup of chopped nuts of your choice
- Berries or fruits of your choic e
- 1 teaspoon baking soda
- ½ cup of brown flaxseed meal
- 1 ½ teaspoons of cinnamon powder
- ½ cup of honey or maple syrup
- Any optional flavorings
- A pinch of salt

DIRECTIONS:

1. Preheat oven to 300 degrees F. Line a biscuit tray with parchment paper.

2. Mix the oatmeal, chopped nuts, flaxseed meal and cinnamon powder together - except the salt.

3. Mix them up nicely with your hands and set the mixture aside. The ground flaxseed is being used because there is marijuana infused-oil in this recipe, and the ground flaxseed will help absorb any of the extra oil.

4. If the weed-infused coconut oil is in the solid state, just heat it in a microwave until it melts into liquid oil. Put the oil into a bowl and add the honey or maple syrup, salt and flavorings to it and mix it well. You can use whatever flavor essences you want depending on your taste - for instance, vanilla, strawberry, pineapple etc.

5. Once the liquid mixture is ready, you can add it to the dry mix that you prepared earlier. Toss and mix everything using spoons, and put the combined mixture into the tray lined with parchment paper. Spread the entire mixture evenly in the tray without pressing down on it.

6. Pop this mix into the preheated oven for about 20 to 30 minutes, and let it cook until it is golden brown. You may check on it after 10 minutes and take it out to stir the mixture around a bit. Then put the mixture back into the oven for 15 to 20 minutes more until you find it becoming golden brown.

7. Take it out and stir in any fresh or dry fruits you like such as berries or other fruit segments. Once it cools a bit, you can shape the granola mix into bars with your hands. Once the bars are done, leave them to cool properly, and your weed granola bars are done! You can store them easily in boxes or bags; they make a great breakfast or snack.

CANNABIS NO-BAKE TOFFEE COOKIES

INGREDIENTS:

- 1 tablespoon cannabis butter
- 3 cups quick-cooking oats
- 1 cup peanut butter
- 1/2 cup bittersweet chocolate chips
- 1/2 cup semisweet chocolate chips
- 1/2 cup toffee bits, plus more for sprinkling
- 1/2 teaspoon kosher salt

DIRECTIONS:

1. Line a baking sheet with wax paper. Combine the oats, peanut butter, bitter and semisweet chocolate chips, toffee bits, cannabis butter and salt in a medium saucepan. Cook over medium heat, stirring frequently, until the chocolate chips melt, 3 to 5 minutes.

2. Scoop heaping tablespoons of batter onto the baking sheet, and sprinkle each cookie with extra toffee bits.

3. Freeze for 15 minutes before serving. The cookies can be stored in the refrigerator in an air-tight container for 1 week.

CANNABIS CHOCOLATE BIRTHDAY CAKE

INGREDIENTS:

- 1/2 cup of cannabis butter
- 8 heaping tablespoons cocoa, plus more for dusting
- 4 cups all-purpose flour
- 4 cups sugar
- 1/2 teaspoon salt
- 2 cups boiling water
- 1 cup buttermilk
- 2 teaspoons baking soda
- 2 teaspoons vanilla extract
- 4 whole eggs, beaten

For Frosting :

- 3 cups heavy cream
- 24 ounces semisweet chocolate, broken into pieces
- 2 teaspoons vanilla extract

DIRECTIONS:

For Cake:

1. Preheat the oven to 350 degrees F. Heavily grease and dust four 9-inch round cake pans with cocoa.

2. In a mixing bowl, combine the flour, sugar and salt.

3. In a saucepan, melt the cannabis butter on very low heat. Add the cocoa. Stir together. Add the boiling water; allow the mixture to simmer on low for 30 seconds, and then turn off the heat. Pour over the flour mixture and stir lightly to cool.

4. Combine the buttermilk, baking soda, vanilla and beaten eggs. Stir the buttermilk mixture into the butter/chocolate mixture.

5. Divide the batter among the prepared cake pans and bake for 20 minutes.

6. Cool completely before icing. Refrigerate the layers after cooling for best results.

For Frosting :

1. Heat the cream until very hot, and then pour over the chocolate pieces. Stir to completely melt, and then pour into the bowl of an electric mixer. Refrigerate to cool.

2. Once completely cooled, add the vanilla and beat with an electric mixer until light and airy.

3. Frost the cake in between each layer, on the top and around the sides.

CANNABIS BANANA MUFFINS

INGREDIENTS:

- 1/4 cup cannabis oil
- 2 1/2 cups unbleached all-purpose flour
- 1/2 teaspoon baking soda
- 3/4 cup dark brown sugar
- 1/4 teaspoon ground cinnamon
- 2 cups smashed bananas (about 4 to 6 bananas)
- 1/2 cup milk
- 2 large eggs, at room temperature
- 1/8 teaspoon fine salt
- 1/2 teaspoon pure vanilla extract
- 3/4 cups chopped walnut s

DIRECTIONS:

1. Preheat the oven to 350 degrees F. Lightly brush a 12-muffin tin with butter and set aside.

2. Whisk the flour, baking soda, brown sugar and cinnamon together in a medium bowl, set aside.

3. Whisk the banana, cannabis oil, milk, eggs, salt and vanilla in a large measuring cup with a spout or another bowl.

4. Make a small well in the center of the dry ingredients. Pour wet ingredients into the center; then stir with a wooden spoon until the dry ingredients are moistened but still lumpy. Do not overmix the batter or your muffins will become dense. Gently stir in the nuts. Divide the batter evenly into the muffin tin.

5. Bake until golden brown, about 25 minutes, rotating the pan halfway through the cooking. (Insert a toothpick into the center of a muffin to check if it is done. Toothpick should come out clean.)

6. Cool muffins in the pan on a rack for a couple minutes. Turn the muffins out of the pan and cool on the rack. Serve warm or at room temperature.

CANNABIS COCONUT CREME BRÛLÉE

INGREDIENTS:

- 2 tablespoons cannabis coconut oil
- 1 cup unsweetened coconut milk
- 1 cup heavy cream
- 1 teaspoon imitation coconut extract
- 4 large eggs
- 8 to 9 tablespoons sugar

DIRECTIONS:

1. Preheat the oven to 325 degrees F.

2. Combine the coconut milk, cream and coconut extract in a small saucepan over medium-high heat and bring to a boil. Once at a boil, remove from the heat. Add coconut oil

3. Meanwhile, whisk together the eggs and 5 tablespoons sugar in a bowl until combined.

4. Slowly whisk the heated cream mixture into the eggs, stirring constantly.

5. Divide the mixture among six, heat-safe 5-ounce coffee mugs or oven-safe ramekins, filling them about 3/4 of the way up. Put them in a baking dish, and add enough warm water to the baking dish so that it comes halfway up the sides of the coffee mugs.

6. Bake until the center is nearly set. Baking time will depend on the height of your coffee mug or ramekin. Bake time is 10 minutes for every 1/2 inch of height. For a 1-inch vessel, bake the creme brulees about 20 minutes. For a 2-inch vessel, bake the creme brulees about 40 minutes.

7. Remove from the oven and allow to completely cool in the water bath, then refrigerate 15 to 20 minutes before serving.

8. Before serving, sprinkle the tops with a heavy layer of sugar. Use a hand torch or heat under the broiler for 2 to 3 minutes.

CANNABIS TIRAMISU

INGREDIENTS:

- 6 extra-large egg yolks, at room temperature
- 1/4 cup sugar
- 1/2 cup good dark rum, divided
- 1 1/2 cups brewed espresso, divided
- 3 tablespoons cannabis coconut oil
- 16 to 17 ounces mascarpone cheese
- 30 Italian ladyfingers or savoiardi
- Bittersweet chocolate, shaved or grated
- Confectioners' sugar (optional)

DIRECTIONS:

1. Whisk the egg yolks and sugar in the bowl of an electric mixer fitted with the whisk attachment on high speed for about 5 minutes, or until very thick and light yellow. Lower the speed to medium and add 1/4 cup rum, 1/4 cup espresso, 2 tablespoons cannabis coconut oil and the mascarpone. Whisk until smooth.

2. Combine the remaining 1/4 cup rum and 1 1/4 cups espresso with 1 tablespoon cannabis coconut oil in a shallow bowl. Dip 1 side of each ladyfinger in the espresso/rum mixture and line the bottom of a 9x12x2-inch dish. Pour half the espresso cream mixture evenly on top. Dip 1 side of the remaining ladyfingers in the espresso/rum mixture and place them in a second layer in the dish. Pour the rest of the espresso cream over the top. Smooth the top and cover with plastic wrap. Refrigerate overnight.

3. Before serving, sprinkle the top with shaved chocolate and dust lightly with confectioners' sugar, if desired.

CHOCOLATE GANACHE CANNABIS CUPCAKES

INGREDIENTS:

- 1/4 cup cannabis butter
- 1 cup sugar
- 4 extra-large eggs, at room temperatur e
- 16 fluid ounces Hershey's chocolate syrup
- 1 tablespoon pure vanilla extract
- 1 cup all-purpose flour
- 1 teaspoon instant coffee granules

For Ganache:

- 1/2 cup heavy cream
- 8 ounces good-quality, semisweet chocolate chips
- 1/2 teaspoon instant coffee granules

DIRECTIONS:

1. Preheat the oven to 325 degrees F. Line a muffin pan with paper liners.

2. Cream the cannabis butter and sugar in the bowl of an electric mixer fitted with the paddle attachment until light and fluffy. Add the eggs, 1 at a time. Mix in the chocolate syrup and vanilla. Add the flour and coffee granules and mix until just combined. Don't overbeat or the cupcakes will be tough.

3. Scoop the batter into the muffin cups and bake for 30 minutes, or until just set in the middle. Don't overbake! Let cool thoroughly in the muffin pan.

For Ganache:

1. Cook the heavy cream, chocolate chips and instant coffee in the top of a double boiler over simmering water until smooth and warm, stirring occasionally.

2. Dip the tops of the cupcakes into the ganache. Do not refrigerate.

CHOCOLATE CANNA-CUPS RECIPE

INGREDIENTS:

- 1/4 teaspoon of cannabis-infused coconut oil
- 1 tablespoon chocolate morsels

- Nuts and fruit (optional)

DIRECTIONS:

1. Melt cannabis-infused coconut oil and chocolate. (You can melt your canna-coconut oil in the Breville Smart Oven at a 120 degrees. The smart oven maintains a slow, consistent heat, and the cannabinoids are not damaged. Also, burnt chocolate is kind of gross.)

2. Mix well. Ensure that melted chocolate and canna-coconut oil is combined well to result in consistent, even doses.

3. Pour melted cannabis-infused chocolate into a lined mini muffin tin.

4. Refrigerate until firm.

TRICOLOR MARSHMELLOW CEREAL TREATS

INGREDIENTS:

- 1.2 ounces freeze-dried strawberries
- 1.2 ounces freeze-dried blueberries
- 1.2 ounces freeze-dried mangoes
- 9 cups crisp rice cereal
- 1/2 cup (1 stick) plus 1 tablespoon unsalted butter
- 3 tablespoons cannabutter
- 5 ounces mini marshmallow s

DIRECTIONS:

1. Coat a 9-inch square baking dish with baking spray and line with parchment paper, allowing 2 inches of overhang on each side.

2. In a completely dry blender, or in the bowl of a food processor fitted with the metal blade, pulse the strawberries until they become fruit dust.

3. Transfer the pulverized strawberries to a medium bowl, clean the blender or food processor, and repeat, separately, with the blueberries and mangoes, placing each fruit into its own bowl.

4. Add 3 cups of the cereal to each bowl. Toss to coat with the fruit dust.

5. In a small saucepan, melt the unsalted butter and cannabutter over medium-low heat. Gradually add the marshmallows, stirring until they are melted and combined.

6. Divide the marshmallow mixture among the three bowls, stirring well to combine.

7. Using your fingers, press the strawberry layer into the prepared baking dish.

8. Press the blueberry and mango layers into the dish over the strawberry layer.

9. Allow the treats to set at room temperature for a minimum of 30 minutes before removing from baking dish and cutting into bars.

CANNABIS THUMBPRINT TEA COOKIES RECIPE

INGREDIENTS:

- 1 cup (4:20) butter and cannabutter
- 1/3 cup powdered sugar
- 1 teaspoon vanilla
- 1 & 2/3 cups flou r

Fruit Filling:

- 8 oz. jar (your choice) of favorite jam/preserve/jelly, 4:20 vg tincture

Chocolate Filling:

- 12 oz. (your choice) of chocolate, cannabis oil

DIRECTIONS:

1. Pre-heat oven to 350 F.

2. In a large mixing bowl, cream together cannabis butter and powdered sugar until light and fluffy. Fold in vanilla.

3. Mix in flour and place finished dough into refrigerator for 30 min.

4. Line cookie trays with parchment paper. Form dough into 1″ balls, then place onto tray, 12 to a tray. Once the cookies have cooled, use the back of a spoon to make indentations into the cookies that will be filled later. Cook for 8-10 minutes or until golden brown. Let cool completely before filling.

For Fruit Filling:

1. Using your favorite jam/jelly/preserve, place contents of one jar into a medium saucepot on low heat. Add 2 tablespoons of water and heat until warm and manageable, then remove from heat. Stir in 2-3 tablespoons of 4:20 VG Tincture (can be adjusted to your personal levels). Fill each cookie and let sit for 15 minutes before placing in refrigerator for 30 minutes.

For Chocolate Filling:

1. Melt your chocolate of choice 1-2 minutes in microwave, then stir in 2-3 tablespoons 4:20 oil (can be adjusted to your personal levels). Fill each cookie and let sit for 15 minutes before placing into refrigerator for 30 minutes.

NO-BAKE FUDGE

INGREDIENTS:

- 7 cups (2 lbs) powdered sugar
- 1 cup of Hershey's cocoa
- 1 lb (4 sticks) of cannabutter
- 1 teaspoon of vanilla essence
- 1 cup of peanut butte r

DIRECTIONS:

1. Melt the butter and peanut butter in a saucepan or double boiler, and add the vanilla essence

2. In a large bowl, mix together the powdered sugar and cocoa.

3. Add the melted ingredients and mix well

4. Press into a flat pan, and place in the fridge until firm

CHOCOLATE-DIPPED WEED CHERRIES

INGREDIENTS:

- 1 cup dark chocolate chips
- 1 cup milk chocolate chips
- ¼ cup cannabis coconut oil
- 24 cherries with stems (washed and dried; if you use fresh cherries, remember to remove the pit!)

DIRECTIONS:

1. Heat milk chocolate chips, dark chocolate chips and cannabis coconut oil in a microwave safe bowl. Remove and stir every 20 seconds until melted. Chocolate should be warm but not hot.

2. Dip dry cherries by the stems in chocolate, one at a time, allowing excess chocolate to drip back into bowl.

3. Set cherries on a wax paper-lined plate to dry. Repeat until all cherries are coated. Save extra chocolate on the side. (You will dip the cherries again.)

4. Chill cherries in the refrigerator for 1 hour.

5. Warm the chocolate sauce back up and remove cherries from the refrigerator.

6. Dip each cherry in the chocolate sauce for a second time. Return cherries to the refrigerator to chill for 1 hour before serving.

7. Store extra cherries in the refrigerator.

CANNABUTTER POUND CAKE

INGREDIENTS:

- ½ cup cannabutter, softened
- 1 cup real butter, softened

- 1 (8 oz) package cream cheese, softened
- 3 cups white sugar
- 6 eggs
- 3 cups all-purpose flou r
- 1 teaspoon vanilla extract

DIRECTIONS:

1. Heat oven to 325 degrees F. Spray a 9×5 bread pan with nonstick spray.

2. With an electric mixer, mix everything except the flour until combined. Once combined, add flour. Mix until combined.

3. Pour mixture into 9×5 pan. Bake 80 minutes.

4. Let it cool !

CANNABIS TAFFY

INGREDIENTS:

- 1½ mugs cocoa sugar
- ½ glass cannabis corn syrup
- 3 tablespoons cannabutter (or customary margarine)
- 1½ teaspoons salt
- 1½ teaspoons vanilla extract

DIRECTIONS:

1. Join cocoa sugar, corn syrup, cannabutter and water in a pan. Heat, mixing infrequently, until temperature comes to 256 degrees F.

2. Include salt and cannabis corn syrup to pot and blend.

3. Pour blend onto a lubed marble/stone section, and permit to cool until you can securely touch it.

4. Stretch out taffy until it is light in shading, including vanilla extract as you extend.

5. Haul out strings of taffy that are 1 inch in measurement. Oil scissors and softly cut taffy into chomp size pieces.

6. Wrap every individual bit of taffy in wax paper. Twist ends to close.

CANNABIS CORN SYRUP

Time Required: 4 hours (suggested minimum)

INGREDIENTS:

- Vast pot or slow cooker
- 3 glasses light corn syrup

- 1 ounce finely ground cannabis

- Cheesecloth

- Spoo n

- Tupperware holder with cover

- Elastic band (one that will extend around the edge of your Tupperware)

DIRECTIONS:

1. Pour the light corn syrup in the pan or stewing pot, and set on low/medium warmth.

2. Let the syrup warm up until it is hot; however, ensure it doesn't bubble.

3. Add your finely ground cannabis to the hot syrup.

4. Blend the cannabis often as it douses for no less than 4 hours. Try not to give it a chance to bubble.

5. Set up your Tupperware holder by taking 2 sheets of the cheesecloth and securing it over the cover of the dish utilizing the elastic band. Turn heat off and let blend cool down somewhat.

6. Pour the cannabis corn syrup blend gradually over the highest point of the cheesecloth and into the holder. Rehash this progression as important to strain the greater part of the plant from the syrup.

7. Permit syrup to cool. Store the cannabis corn syrup in an impenetrable holder and keep it in a cool, dim spot.

CANNA-BANANA BREAD

Preparation Time: 10-15 minutes- **Cooking Time:** 60 minutes - **Servings:** 4-6

INGREDIENTS:

- ½ cup of soft Cannabutter

- 1 cup of white sugar

- 2 eggs

- 1 teaspoon of vanilla extract

- 1 ½ cup of mashed banana

- 2 cups of flour

- 1 teaspoon of baking soda

DIRECTIONS:

1. Preheat the oven to 350 degrees. Grease a 9 "x 5" loaf tin and dust with flour. Beat the Cannabutter and the sugar until smooth. Add vanilla extract. Beat in the eggs and then the bananas. Stir in flour and baking powder carefully. Pour the bread batter into the pan. Bake in the preheated oven for an hour.

Nutrition:

Calories: 295, Fat: 8.1g, Fiber: 2.3, Carbs: 45g, Protein: 1.8g

RED VELVET CANNA CAKE

Preparation Time: 20 minutes- **Cooking Time:** 35-40 minutes - **Servings**: 20-24
INGREDIENTS:

- 16 ounces of cream cheese
- 4 ounces of butter, softened
- 3 cups of powdered sugar
- 2 ¾ cup of purpose flour
- 1 ¾ cup of white sugar
- 1 ¼ cup of buttermilk
- ¾ cup of canola oil
- ¾ cup canna oil
- 2 eggs
- 1 tablespoon of white vinegar
- 4 teaspoons of red food coloring
- 3 teaspoons of vanilla extract
- 2 teaspoons of cocoa powder
- 1 teaspoon of baking soda
- ¼ teaspoon of salt

DIRECTIONS:

1. Before you do anything preheat the oven to 325 F. Beat the eggs with canna oil, canola oil, 1 teaspoon of vanilla extract, buttermilk and vinegar in a large mixing bowl Stir the flour with white sugar, cocoa powder, baking soda and salt. Add the mixture gradually to the buttermilk while whisking all the time until no lumps are found. Add the liquid food coloring and stir in the batter until you get a dark red batter. Pour the batter into 3 lined up and greased cake pans then cook them in the oven for 34 to 36 min. Once the time is up, allow the cakes to lose heat completely. In the meantime, beat the butter in a large mixing bowl until they become soft. Add the sugar gradually while beating all the time, followed by the cream cheese until the mix becomes soft and fluffy. Add the vanilla extract then mix them well to make the icing. Level the cakes with a sharp bread knife to make them equal with the same thickness and size. Place some icing in the middle of a cake stand and place it on top of it a cake. Spread some frosting on it, then top it with the second cake and repeat the process to with the third cake. Cover the whole cake with the rest of the frosting, then decorate it the way you desire and refrigerate it for 30 min or more. Serve your cake and enjoy it.

Nutrition:

Calories: 288, Fat: 8.7g, Fiber: 2.1g, Carbs: 54g, Protein: 1.8g

CHERRY- CRANBERRY GINGER CAKE

Preparation Time: 15 minutes- **Cooking Time:** 35 -40 minutes - **Servings**: 4-6

INGREDIENTS:

- 1½ cups Dark Cherries drained, chopped-set aside
- 2 cups whole wheat white cake flour
- ½ teaspoon ground ginger
- 2 tablespoons chopped crystallized ginger
- ¼ teaspoon salt
- 1½ teaspoons baking powder
- ½ cup cranberries
- ½ cup apricots, chopped
- ¾ cup canna milk
- 2 eggs
- ¼ cup stevia
- 3 tablespoons molasses
- ¼ cup coconut oil softened

DIRECTIONS:

1. Prepare a lightly greased and lined with parchment paper 9-inch cake pan. In a bowl, put all dry ingredients together and mix well. Then, in another bowl, put all wet ingredients and mix with a whisk. Combine egg mixture and flour and blend Fold in cherries and bake at 350°F for30-35 minutes.

Nutrition:

Calories: 256, Fat: 6.5g, Fiber: 4g, Carbs: 41.2g, Protein: 1.7g

PEACH JELLY ROLL

Preparation Time: 15-20 minutes - **Cooking Time:** 60 minutes - **Servings**: 6-8

INGREDIENTS:

- 2¼ cups whole wheat pastry flour
- ¼ cup wheat bran, unprocessed
- ½ teaspoon baking powder
- ¼ teaspoon baking soda
- ½ teaspoon salt
- ½ cup canna coconut oil, slightly softened but still firm
- ¾ cup yogurt
- ¼ cup milk
- 8 cups peaches, thinly sliced
- 1 cup dates, minced

- ¼ cup honey

DIRECTIONS:

1. In a bowl, combine all the prepared dry ingredients and mix well. Mix in coconut oil and slowly add other wet ingredients except for peaches, dates and honey, for the remaining three ingredients, mix all of it and set aside. Divide dough in two and roll each on a floured surface into a rectangle shape

2. Split peaches in half and top each section of rolled dough, leaving edges free. Roll up without letting peaches fall out and pinch to seal. In a greased pan, bake, covered at 350°F for 30 minutes and uncovered for an additional 30 minutes.

Nutrition:

Calories: 210, Fat: 6.8g, Fiber: 4.1, Carbs: 34.6g, Protein: 2.1g

SILKY COCONUT CAKE

Preparation Time: 15-20 minutes- **Cooking Time:** 30-40 minutes **- Servings**: 6-8

INGREDIENTS:

- 2 cups whole wheat cake flour
- 2 teaspoons baking powder
- ½ cup toasted wheat bran
- ½ teaspoon baking soda
- 3 teaspoons lemon zest
- ½ cup of cocoa powder
- ½ teaspoon salt
- 2 large eggs
- ½ cup molasses
- ½ cup dark honey
- ½ cup apple juice
- ½ cup of coconut oil at room temperature
- ¾ cup dark chocolate chips
- Chocolate Frosting (optional)

DIRECTIONS:

1. In a bowl, combine all the prepared dry ingredients and mix well. Same goes with all the wet ingredients, slowly add together using whisk; egg mixture, flour mixture and 1 cup boiling water, a little at a time until totally incorporated; do not over mix Stir in chocolate chips then fold. Pour cake in a lined 12-inch round spring form pan and bake at 350°F for 30-40 minutes until springs back when you press. Cool then frost with chocolate frosting.

Nutrition:

Calories: 245, Fat: 8g, Fiber: 4.3g, Carbs: 30.9g, Protein: 2.6g

CANNABIS STRAWBERRY CAKE

Preparation Time: 20 minutes- **Cooking Time:** 40 minutes - **Servings**: 12

INGREDIENTS:

- Nonstick baking spray
- 10 tablespoons (1¼ sticks) unsalted butter,
- 2 tablespoons Canna-Butter, melted
- 1¼ cups plus 2 tablespoons granulated sugar, divided
- 2 large eggs, lightly beaten
- 1 tablespoon orange juice concentrate
- 2 teaspoons grated orange zest
- ½ teaspoon almond extract
- 1½ cups gluten-free 1-to-1 baking flour
- ½ cup plus 1 tablespoon strawberry jam, divided
- 1 cup slivered or sliced almonds
- 1½ cups vanilla Greek yogurt

DIRECTIONS:

1. Preheat the oven to 340°F.Using a nonstick spray or butter and flour, Coat a 9-inch square baking pan. In a large bowl, combine the melted butter and 1¼ cups of sugar. Stir in the beaten eggs and mix well. Stir in the orange juice concentrate, zest, and almond extract. Stir in the flour until just mixed. Pour the batter into the prepared pan. Using a knife, swirl ½ cup of the jam into the batter toward the center. Sprinkle with the almonds, then the remaining 2 tablespoons sugar. Bake until golden and set, 35 to 40 minutes. Once completely cooled slice into 12 equal pieces. In a small bowl, combine the yogurt with the remaining 1 tablespoon jam and place a dollop on each slice.

Nutrition:

Calories: 341, Fat: 8.1g, Fiber: 6g, Carbs: 41.7g, Protein: 1.7g

STONER'S LEMON POPPY SEED LOAF

Preparation Time: 20 minutes- **Cooking Time:** 55-65 min - **Servings**: 6-8

INGREDIENTS:

- 1 ¾ cups All-purpose flour
- ¾ cup Cannabis Butter* melted
- 1 tablespoon poppy seeds

- 1 cup Granulated sugar
- 1 teaspoon Baking powder
- 2/3 cup Milk
- 2 Eggs 1 teaspoon Vanilla
- 1 tablespoon Lemon zest
- ½ teaspoon Salt
- For the Glaze
- **½ cup icing sugar**
- 1 tablespoon Lemon juice

DIRECTIONS:

1. Preheat oven the oven to 350 F. Grease a 9 × 5 in. Loaf pan. Mix flour with sugar, poppy seeds, lemon zest, baking powder and salt in a bowl. Cream the Cannabis Butter* with milk, eggs and vanilla in a large bowl, using a whisk or an electric mixer on medium, until smooth and creamy in texture, Then, blend in flour mixture and mix until just combined. Don't over-mix. Pour the mixture into a loaf pan. Bake and check if it is cooked by inserting a wooden skewer or toothpick in the center of the loaf and when it comes out clean, around 55 to 65 min. Transfer pan to a cooling rack, and let stand 10 min. Meanwhile, do the glaze, Whisk icing sugar with lemon juice in a small bowl. Brush glaze over warm loaf. Let stand until loaf is cool, about 2 hours.

Nutrition:

Calories: 290, Fat: 3.5, Fiber: 4.1, Carbs: 45g, Protein: 4.6g

CHOCO-ESPRESSO SPELT CAKE

Preparation Time: 30 minutes- **Cooking Time:** 1 hr. - **Servings**: 8-12

INGREDIENTS:

- 2 cups spelt flour
- 3/4 cup cannabutter
- 3/4 cup cocoa powder
- 1 cup packed dark brown sugar
- 2 large eggs
- 1 cup boiling-hot water
- 1 1/2 tablespoons instant espresso powder
- 1 teaspoon baking soda
- 1 1/2 cups dates (12 to 14), pitted and coarsely chopped
- 2 teaspoons baking powder
- 3/4 teaspoon salt

- 1 1/2 teaspoons vanilla extract

DIRECTIONS:

1. Preheat oven to 350F. Grease spring form pan, then lightly dust with cocoa powder, removing out excess. Mix together boiling-hot water, espresso powder, vanilla, and baking soda in a bowl, then add dates, mashing lightly with a fork, and slightly simmer then cool down to room temperature, about 10 minutes. Blend together spelt flour, cocoa powder, baking powder, and salt in another bowl. Cream together canna butter and brown sugar until pale and fluffy. Put in the eggs one at a time. Add in date mixture and add the flour a little at a time, mixing until just combined. Spoon batter into a spring form pan, smoothing top, and bake until a wooden pick or skewer inserted into the center comes out clean, about 50 minutes to 1 hour. Cool down the cake by transferring it to a rack for a few minutes, then remove side of the pan and cool cake on rack. Serve cake warm or at room temperature.

Nutrition:

Calories: 280, Fat: 6.1g, Fiber: 4.3g, Carbs: 39.1g, Protein: 5g

CANNA CINNAMON COFFEE CAKE

Preparation Time: 20 minutes- **Cooking Time:** 30 minutes - **Servings**: 4-6

INGREDIENTS:

- 1 1/4 cups flour (cannabis flour extra potency)
- 1/4 cup cannabutter
- 1/2 cup sugar
- 1/4 cup sour cream
- 1/3 cup canna milk or regular milk
- 2 eggs, slightly beaten
- 2 tsp. baking powder
- 1.5 tsp. cinnamon
- Topping:
- 1/3 cup flour
- 1/3 cup brown sugar
- 1/4 cup cannabutter
- 1 tsp. cinnamon powder

DIRECTIONS:

1. First, preheat the oven to375 degrees Fahrenheit, subsequently combining all ingredients for the cake batter in a large mixing bowl. After thoroughly mixing, pour the batter into an 8 or 9-inch greased or buttered pan. After this, combine the flour and brown sugars for the topping in a big bowl, mixing in the cannabutter and cinnamon after. Mix until it becomes chunky and crumbly. Spread over the batter and

bake for 28-30 minutes.

Nutrition:

Calories: 311, Fat: 7,5g, Fiber: 3g, Carbs: 40.1g, Protein: 5g

CANNA APPLE PECAN SPACE CAKE

Preparation Time: 20 minutes- **Cooking Time:** 45 minutes - **Servings**: 4-6

INGREDIENTS:

- 1 cup flour
- 1/2 cup whole wheat flour
- 1/4 tsp. cinnamon
- 1/2 tsp. baking soda
- 1/2 tsp. nutmeg
- 1/2 tsp. salt
- 1 egg
- 1 cup granulated
- 2/3 cup canna oil
- 1/2 cup pecans chopped
- 2 apples, peeled and grated
- 1 gala apple, thinly sliced
- 15 pecan halves

For the glaze:

- 1/4 cup brown sugar
- 2 tsp. cannabis oil
- 2 tsp. water

DIRECTIONS:

1. Heat your oven to 325 degrees Fahrenheit. Lightly coat a 9-inch spring form pan with nonstick cooking spray, In a medium bowl, combine the cinnamon, flours, baking soda, nutmeg and salt until blended. Whisk sugar and egg with the 2/3 cup cannabis-infused olive oil in a bowl. Stir the flour mixture into the egg mixture, and add the chopped pecans and grated apples. Scrape into the prepared pan and flatten the top of it, Arrange the apple slices on top of the edge of the cake, and arrange the pecan halves in one layer in the center.

2. Make the glaze in a small bowl. Mix together the brown sugar and the 2 tsp. olive oil and water and microwave in thirty-second intervals until the brown sugar is melted. Brush the apples and pecan with half of the glaze and save the rest.

3. Bake in the center of the oven until a toothpick when inserted in the middle of the cake comes out clean.

Remove the pan out of the oven and brush the top of the warm cake with the rest of the glaze. Gently remove the cake from the base then serve.

Nutrition:

Calories: 290, Fat: 7.2g, Fiber: 4.1, Carbs: 46g, Protein: 3.4g

CANNA CARROT MUFFINS

Preparation Time: 15 minutes- **Cooking Time:** 25-30 minutes - **Servings**: 10-12

INGREDIENTS:

- 1¾ cups flour
- 1 teaspoon salt
- 1 teaspoon cinnamon
- 1teaspoon ground ginger
- ½ teaspoon grated nutmeg
- ¼ teaspoon baking soda
- ⅛ teaspoon baking powder
- 1 cup maple syrup
- ½ cup solid CBD Coconut Oil melted, or ¼ cup CBD Oil mixed with ¼ cup vegetable oil
- ½ cup milk
- 1 tablespoon fresh lemon juice
- 1 teaspoon vanilla extract
- 2 cups grated carrot
- ½ cup crushed pineapple, drained
- ½ cup each raisin, coconut, and pecans (or any nuts you like)

DIRECTIONS:

1. Preheat the oven to 350°F. Line two 12-cup muffin tins with muffin papers or grease and flour the tins. In a large bowl, combine the flour, salt, cinnamon, ginger, nutmeg, baking soda, and baking powder. In a separate bowl, combine the maple syrup, coconut oil, milk, lemon juice, and vanilla. Combine both the wet and dry ingredients then fold it gently until just combined (over mixing makes the muffins tough). Fold in the carrots, pineapple, raisins, coconut, and pecans. Fill the prepared muffin tins two-thirds full. Let the cake bake for around 25 minutes or more or until a toothpick inserted into the center of a muffin comes out clean. Let them cool a little before serving.

Nutrition:

Calories: 200, Fat: 5.1g, Fiber: 2tgg, Carbs: 25.8g, Protein: 1.2g

RUM RAISIN CUPCAKES

INGREDIENTS:

- Rum Raisins
- ¼ cup dark rum
- ½ cup golden raisins
- Cupcakes
- 1 cup all-purpose flour
- 1¼ teaspoons baking powder
- ¼ teaspoon ground cinnamon
- ⅛ teaspoon ground allspice
- ⅛ teaspoon freshly grated nutmeg
- ½ cup cannabutter, slightly softened
- 2 tablespoons unsalted butter, slightly softened
- ¾ cup firmly packed light brown sugar
- 3 large eggs
- 1 tablespoon pure vanilla extract
- ¼ teaspoon pure rum extract
- Sweet Cream Frosting
- ¼ cup unsalted butter, slightly softened
- ½ cup heavy cream
- 2 cups powdered sugar, sifted
- ⅛ teaspoon salt

DIRECTIONS:

1. Prepare the rum raisins: In a small saucepan, warm the rum over low heat. Blend in the raisins and put it away from heat. Put the mix in a bowl, and then cover it with a saran wrap and let sit at room temperature for at least 6 hours or overnight. Prepare the cupcakes: Bring the temperature of your oven to 180c Put paper liners in the muffin tin. Ina medium bowl, stir together the flour, baking powder, cinnamon, allspice, and nutmeg. Set aside. Ina large bowl using an electric mixer, beat together the cannabutter, regular butter, and brown sugar on medium to high speed until you see that it becomes light and cloudlike, gradually add eggs, beating well after each addition. Beat in the vanilla and rum extracts. Reduce the speed mixer to low, add the flour mixture, and mix until just combined. Fold in the rum raisins and any remaining liquid. Scoop up the cupcake batter into the pan. Bake it for about 20 to 25 minutes, or until golden brown and a toothpick inserted into the center of a cupcake comes out clean. Let cool in the tin for 5 minutes, and then transfer to a wire rack to cool completely. Cupcakes without frosting can be stored up to 3 months. Prepare the sweet cream frosting: In a medium bowl using an electric mixer, beat the butter on medium speed until creamy. Lower down the speed to medium and add the cream and 1 cup of the powdered sugar; beat until well combined. Slowly add the remaining1 cup

sugar and the salt. Put the frosting to a piping bag fitted with the tip of your choice and frost the cupcakes, or simply frost them with a butter knife or small offset spatula. Store the frosted cupcakes in an airtight container in the refrigerator for up to 1 week.

Nutrition:

Calories: 215, Fat: 5g, Fiber: 4.1, Carbs: 35.6g, Protein: 2g

HOT GANJA CHOCOLATE CUPCAKES

Preparation Time: 10 minutes- **Cooking Time:** 20-25 minutes - **Servings**: 2-4

INGREDIENTS:

- ½ Cup all-purpose flour
- 1 tsp. Baking Powder
- Pinch Salt
- 1/3 Cup Cocoa
- ½-1 t Hot Red Pepper Flakes
- 2 tbsp. canna oil
- Scant ½ Cup of milk
- ½ tsp. Vanilla
- ¼ tsp. Apple Cider Vinegar
- ¼ Cup Sugar

DIRECTIONS:

1. Preheat oven to 365°. Combine Flour, Baking Powder, Salt and Sugar. Whisk! Add wet ingredients and whisk until completely smooth. Fill 4-5 cupcake liners 2/3 full. Bake for 20 minutes or until a toothpick comes out clean. Allow to cool completely before frosting.

Nutrition:

Calories: 187, Fat: 4.3g, Fiber: 2g, Carbs: 29.6g, Protein: 1g

FRENCH TOAST CUPCAKES

Preparation Time: 20 minutes- **Cooking Time:** 20-25 minutes - **Servings**: 12

INGREDIENTS:

- Topping
- ¼ cup all-purpose flour
- ¼ cup of sugar
- 2½ tablespoons unsalted butter, cut into ½-inch pieces and chilled
- ½ teaspoon ground cinnamon

* ¼ cup chopped pecans
* Cupcakes
* 1½ cups all-purpose flour
* 1 cup of sugar
* 1½ teaspoons baking powder
* 1 teaspoon ground cinnamon
* ½ teaspoon ground allspice
* ¼ teaspoon freshly grated nutmeg
* ½ teaspoon salt
* ½ cup cannabutter slightly softened
* ½ cup sour cream
* 2 large eggs
* ½ teaspoon maple extract
* 4 slices bacon

DIRECTIONS:

1. First the topping must be prepared. In a medium bowl, blend in sugar, flour, cinnamon, walnuts and butter. Using your fingers, blend in the butter until there are no pieces bigger than a little pea. Cover and refrigerate until prepared to use. Set up the cupcakes: Preheat your stove to 350°F. Line a 12-cup biscuit tin with paper liners. In an enormous bowl, whisk together the flour, sugar, preparing powder, cinnamon, allspice, nutmeg, and salt. Put in a safe spot. In a huge bowl utilizing an electric blender, beat together the cannabutter, cream, eggs, and maple syrup on medium speed until the blend is mixed well. Lessen the blender speed to low and include the flour blend. Beat until simply consolidated. Fill each well of the biscuit tin 2/3 full, bake it for around 20 to 25 minutes or until a toothpick embedded into the focal point of a cupcake tells the truth. While the cupcakes are heating, cook the bacon as how you like it done. Move to a paper towel to drip the excess oil and let cool. Cupcakes must be chilled off in the tin for around 15 minutes. At that point, move to a wire rack to cool totally. Cut the bacon into 12 pieces and press a piece into the top of each muffin. For storing muffins in the freezer, seal it tightly, and it can last up to 3 months, just omit the bacon. Reheat in the toaster oven for extra deliciousness.

Nutrition:

Calories: 190, Fat: 5g, Fiber: 3g, Carbs: 28.8g, Protein: 1.7g

CANNABIS HUMMINGBIRD CUPCAKES

Preparation Time: 10-15 minutes - **Cooking Time:** 15-20 minutes - **Servings**: 12

INGREDIENTS:

* 2 large ripe bananas, mashed

- 1 cup of all-purpose
- 1/2 tsp. baking powder
- 1/3 cup pineapple (crushed (do not drain)
- 1/2 tsp. baking soda
- 1/2 tsp. ground cinnamon
- 1/4 tsp. salt
- ½ cup cannabutter, at room temperature
- 1/2 cup sugar
- 2 large eggs
- 1 tsp. pure vanilla extract
- 1/2 cup chopped pecans
- 1 cup unsweetened desiccated coconut
- 1/2 cup golden raisins (optional)
- Cream Cheese Frosting
- 8 ounces cream cheese, at room temperature
- 1/4 cup butter, at room temperature
- 3 cups powdered sugar
- 2 teaspoons vanilla extract

DIRECTIONS:

1. Preheat your oven to 350 degrees placing the rack in the center. Line a 12-cup muffin pan with cupcake liners in preparation. Combine the bananas and pineapples in a bowl. Mash together with the back of a fork and set aside. Whisk or beat together the flour, baking powder, baking soda, cinnamon and salt in a separate medium bowl. Add the cannabutter and the sugar to a large bowl. Beat with a whisk until the mixture is fluffy and light. Gradually put the eggs and then the vanilla extract. Add the dry ingredients into the wet by scoopfuls and beat until thoroughly combined.

2. Stir in the pineapple and bananas, being careful not to over-mix. Fold in the pecans, coconut and golden raisins (if using). Pour batter into the liners, working to fill at least 2/3 of the way. Put it inside the oven and let it bake for around 30 to 40 minutes. The signs of completed cupcakes will include a toothpick that comes out clean and an outwardly golden appearance.

3. Remove from the oven and place on a wire rack to cool. Once this is achieved, use a small spatula or kitchen knife to frost tops of each cupcake. Top with finely chopped pecans.

4. Frosting (Cream-cheese)

5. Put the cream cheese and the butter in a bowl then and beat together with a whisk until very smooth and no lumps. Then add in the vanilla extract and fine sugar, continuously beating until it is light and smooth.

Nutrition:

Calories: 216, Fat: 3.1g, Fiber: 1.4g, Carbs: 56g, Protein: 4

KIRSCH CHOCOLATE MUFFINS

Preparation Time: 15 minutes- **Cooking Time:** 20-25 minutes - **Servings**: 6-8

INGREDIENTS:

- 1/2 tsp. baking soda
- 1/2 cup of cannabutter
- ½ cup of roughly cut dark chocolate
- 3/4 cup of brown sugar
- 1/4 cup of either unsweetened cocoa powder (Dutch cocoa works too)
- 3/4 cup of milk
- 1 1/4 cups of self-rising flour
- 2 eggs
- 15 ounces of dark cherries in syrup (thawed, drained, whatever the preference)
- 1 tbsp. cocoa
- Extra 1 tsp. icing sugar

DIRECTIONS:

1. Set the oven to 350°F. Prepare a 12-hole muffin tray with liners. Cream the butter and sugar together, adding a single egg at a time. Take the baking soda, the cocoa, and the flour and sift together with the butter mix from before. Finish up by combining with the milk, chocolate, and cherries. Try to fill each cupcake tin to approximately ¾ full and place in the preheated oven for 20-25 minutes. A sign that cupcakes are done is by doing the clean toothpick test. Once it is cooked, put it away from heat and let cool while the icing is made. Frost and enjoy it!

Nutrition:

Calories: 196, Fat: 4.2g, Fiber: 1.8, Carbs: 30.6g, Protein: 1.1g

CANNA- BANANA CRUMBLE MUFFINS

Preparation Time: 10-15 minutes- **Cooking Time:** 18-20 minutes - **Servings**: 8-10

INGREDIENTS:

- 1 ½ cups flour
- 1/3 cup cannabis butter
- 3 mashed bananas
- 3/4 cup cane sugar
- 1/3 cup packed brown sugar

- 1 tsp. baking soda
- 1 tsp. baking powder
- 1/2 tsp. table salt
- 1 egg
- 2 tbsp. flour
- 1 tbsp. butter
- 1/8 tsp. ground cinnamon

DIRECTIONS:

1. Bring the heat of your oven to 350 f. and lightly butter a 10-cup muffin tray. Get out a large mixing bowl and mix the 1.5 cups flour, baking soda, baking powder and salt. In a separate bowl, mix the mashed bananas, egg, cane sugar and 1/3 cup melted cannabis butter. Stir this mixture into the first mixture until just blended. Spread this batter evenly into the greased or buttered muffin cups. In another bowl, combine the brown sugar, cinnamon and 2 tbsp. Flour. Cut in 1 tbsp. Butter. Sprinkle this mixture over the muffin batter in the trays. Bake 18 - 20 minutes; allow cooling on a wire rack and enjoying.

Nutrition:

Calories: 210, Fat: 6g, Fiber: 2.4, Carbs: 35g, Protein: 1.7 g

CANNABIS PANCAKES

INGREDIENTS:

- 1/2 cup cannabis milk
- 1/2 cup whole milk
- 1 cup all purpose flour
- 2 tablespoons white sugar
- 2 teaspoons baking powder
- 1 egg beaten
- 2 tablespoons vegetable oil
- 1 teaspoon salt

DIRECTIONS :

1. In a large bowl, mix flour, sugar, baking powder and salt. Make a well in the center, and pour in cannabis milk, whole milk, egg and oil. Mix until smooth.

2. Heat a lightly oiled griddle or frying pan over medium-high heat. Pour or scoop the batter onto the griddle, using approximately 1/4 cup for each pancake. Brown on both sides and serve hot.

3. Serve the cannabis pancakes.

CANNABIS CARROT CAKE

INGREDIENTS:

- 1 cup cannabis milk
- 3 eggs
- 1 1/2 cups sugar
- 2 cups all-purpose flour
- 2 teaspoons baking soda
- 2 cups shredded carrots
- 1 cup flaked coconut
- 1 cup chopped walnuts
- 1 can crushed pineapple with juice
- 1 cup raisins
- 2 teaspoons vanilla extract
- 2 teaspoons ground cinnamon
- 1/4 teaspoon salt

DIRECTIONS:

1. Preheat oven to 350 degrees F.

2. Grease and flour an 8×12 inch pan .

3. In a medium bowl, sift together flour, baking soda, salt and cinnamon. Set aside.

4. In a large bowl, combine eggs, cannabis milk, oil, sugar and vanilla. Mix well. Add flour mixture and mix well.

5. In a medium bowl, combine shredded carrots, coconut, walnuts, pineapple and raisins.

6. Using a large wooden spoon or a very heavy whisk, add carrot mixture to batter and fold in well.

7. Pour into prepared 8×12 inch pan, and bake for 1 hour. Check for doneness with toothpick.

8. Allow to cool for at least 20 minutes before serving.

MARIJUANA CHEESECAKE

INGREDIENTS:

- 2 tablespoons cannabis butter
- 1 tablespoon normal butter
- 24 oreo cookies, divided
- 3 (250 grams) Philadelphia cream cheese packets
- 3/4 cup sugar
- 1 teaspoon vanilla 3 eggs

DIRECTIONS:

1. Preheat oven to 330 degrees F.

2. Place 16 of the cookies in resealable plastic bag. Flatten bag to remove excess air, then seal bag. Finely crush cookies by rolling a rolling pin across the bag .

3. Place in bowl. Add butter; mix well. Press firmly onto bottom of 9-inch springform pan.

4. Beat cream cheese, sugar and vanilla in large bowl with electric mixer on medium speed until well blended. Add eggs, 1 at a time, beating just until blended after each addition.

5. Chop or crush remaining 8 cookies. Gently stir half of the chopped cookies into cream cheese batter. Pour over prepared crust; sprinkle with the remaining chopped cookies.

6. Bake 45 minutes or until center is almost set. Cool. Refrigerate 3 hours or overnight. Cut into 12 pieces. Store leftover cheesecake in refrigerator.

CANNABIS GINGERBREAD

INGREDIENTS:

- 1/4 cup cannabis butter
- 1/4 cup normal butter
- One egg
- One cup molasses
- 2 1/2 cups all-purpose flour
- 1 1/2 teaspoons bakins soda
- 1 teaspoon ground cumin
- 1 teaspoon ground ginger
- 1/2 teaspoon salt
- 1 cup hot water

DIRECTIONS:

1. Preheat oven to 330 degrees F.

2. Grease and flour a 9-inch square pan.

3. In a large bowl, cream together the sugar and butter. Beat in the egg, and mix in the molasses.

4. In a bowl, sift together the flour, baking soda, salt, cinnamon, ginger and cloves. Blend into the creamed mixture. Stir in the hot water. Pour into the prepared pan.

5. Bake 1 hour in the preheated oven until a knife inserted in the center comes out clean. Allow to cool in pan before serving.

CHOCOLATE CANNABIS BAR

INGREDIENTS:

- 1/4 cup cannabis butter

- 4 cups chocolate

DIRECTIONS:

1. Melt the chocolate in a clean, dry bowl set over a pan of barely simmering water. If you want to temper the chocolate, add your cannabis butter.

2. Once the chocolate is melted (and tempered, if tempering the chocolate), remove the bowl from the pan and wipe the moisture off the bottom of the bowl.

3. Pour or spoon a layer of chocolate into your molds. Rap them on the counter a few times to distribute the chocolate evenly and release any air bubbles; then working quickly, top with any kinds of nuts, dried fruits or other ingredients that you wish and press them in slightly.

4. (You can also stir ingredients into the chocolate, such as toasted nuts, seeds, crisped rice cereal, snipped marshmallows or other ingredients, then pour the mixture into the molds.)

5. Immediately put the bars in the refrigerator until firm. If tempered chocolate is used, it shouldn't take more than five minutes for them to firm up. Otherwise, the chocolate will take longer.

CANNABIS BASIC MUFFINS

INGREDIENTS:

- 1/4 cup melted cannabis butter
- 2 cups all-purpose flour
- 3 teaspoons baking powder
- 1/2 teaspoon salt
- 3/4 cup white sugar
- 1 egg
- 1 cup milk

DIRECTIONS:

1. Preheat oven to 350 degrees F.

2. Melt cannabis butter on very low temperature .

3. Stir together the flour, baking powder, salt and sugar in a large bowl. Make a well in the center. In a small bowl or 2 cup measuring cup, beat egg with a fork. Stir in milk and cannabis butter. Pour all at once into the well in the flour mixture.

4. Mix quickly and lightly with a fork until moistened.The batter will be lumpy. Pour the batter into paper lined muffin pan cups.

5. Bake for 25 minutes or until golden.

CHEWY CHOCOLATE CHIP WEED

COOKIES

INGREDIENTS:

- 1/4 cup softened cannabis butter
- 1/2 cup softened normal butter
- 2 cups all-purpose flour
- 1/2 teaspoon baking soda
- 1/2 teaspoon salt
- One cup brown sugar
- 1/2 cup white suga r
- 1 tablespoon vanilla extract
- 1 egg
- 1 egg yolk
- 2 cups chocolate chips

DIRECTIONS:

1. Preheat the oven to 325 degrees F.

2. Grease cookie sheets or line with parchment paper.

3. In a bowl, sift together the flour, baking soda and salt; set aside.

4. In a medium bowl, cream together the cannabis butter, normal butter, brown sugar and white sugar until well blended. Beat in the vanilla, egg and egg yolk until light and creamy.

5. Mix in the sifted ingredients until just blended. Stir in the chocolate chips by hand using a wooden spoon.

6. Drop cookie dough 1/4 cup at a time onto the prepared cookie sheets. Cookies should be about 3 inches apart.

7. Bake for 15 to 17 minutes in the preheated oven, or until the edges are lightly toasted. Cool on baking sheets for a few minutes before transferring to wire racks to cool completely.

PEANUT BUTTER BUD BARS

INGREDIENTS:

- ½ cup cannabutter, melted
- ½ cup regular butter, melted
- 1 tablespoon decarb seasoning
- 2 cups Graham cracker crumbs
- 2 cups powdered sugar
- 1 cup + 4 tablespoons creamy peanut butter

- 1 ½ cups semisweet chocolate chips

DIRECTIONS:

1. In a bowl, mix cannabutter, regular butter, Graham cracker crumbs, powdered sugar and 1 cup creamy peanut butter until combined. Press evenly into bottom of 9×13 baking pan.

2. In a saucepan and on medium heat, mix the chocolate chips, decarb seasoning and 4 tablespoons peanut butter until melted and combined.

3. Spread the peanut butter mixture evenly on the crust and refrigerate for 2 hours.

4. Cut into 1 inch squares before serving.

CHRONIC APPLE CRISP

INGREDIENTS:

- 10 cups apples, peeled, cored, and sliced
- 1 cup white sugar
- 1 cup + 1 tablespoon all-purpose flour
- 1 teaspoon ground cinnamon
- ½ cup water
- 1 cup quick cooking oats
- 1 cup brown sugar
- ¼ teaspoon baking powder
- ¼ teaspoon baking soda
- ½ cup cannabutter, melted
- 1 ounce cannabis tincture

DIRECTIONS :

1. Heat oven to 350 degrees F. Spread apples evenly in 9×13 inch baking pan

2. In separate dish, mix cinnamon, 1 tablespoon flour and white sugar until combined. Sprinkle mix on apples. Pour water on apples.

3. In separate dish, mix oats, brown sugar, baking powder, baking soda, remaining flour, cannabutter and tincture until combined. Spread mixture evenly on top of apples'

4. Bake for 45 minutes. Serve warm.

SPACE CAKE

INGREDIENTS:

- 1 ¼ cups of baking flour
- 200 CL. of milk

- 2 eggs
- 180 grams of sugar
- ¾ cup butter
- 8 grams of good (light) hash. (You can use Polm or Zero.)

DIRECTIONS:

1. Preheat oven to 200 degrees c

2. Put the butter in the microwave for about 20 seconds until it's a fat paste. Mix the hash with 4/5th of the butter. (Heat up the hash with a lighter and crumble it in the butter.) With the rest of the butter your fatten the baking form so you can get the cake out easy when it's done.

3. Mix the butter (and hash), flour, eggs, milk and sugar (and the possible extra ingredient). Keep on mixing it for a few minutes until it's nice and smooth. If it's too dry: add a little milk. If there is too much liquid, add a little flour.

CANNABIS SUGAR COOKIES

INGREDIENTS:

- 1 cup of cannabis butter
- 1 cup brown sugar
- 1/2 cup white sugar
- 1 large egg
- 1 teaspoon vanilla
- 2 cups all-purpose flour
- 1/2 teaspoon of baking powder
- Pinch or two of salt

DIRECTIONS:

1. Preheat oven to

2. Place the cannabis butter in a large bowl, and beat until it is very light and fluffy .

3. Once fluffy, add sugar, a quarter cup at a time, continuing to vigorously beat the mix.

4. Beat in the large egg and the vanilla flavoring.

5. In a separate small bowl, mix together the baking powder, flour and the pinch of salt.

6. Gradually beat the flour mix into the large bowl until completely mixed together.

7. Divide the finished dough mixture into two halves, wrap each half in plastic wrap, and then refrigerate overnight.

8. Roll each half with a rolling pin on a floured surface; the dough should have a thickness of about ? of an inch.

9. Use a cookie cutter, any shape that you want, and then place the dough shapes onto a prepared cookie sheet at least 1 inch apart.

10. Bake for 10-12 minutes, remove them from the oven when they look golden brown.

11. Leave the cookies to cool before eating.

STRAWBERRY WEED MUFFINS

INGREDIENTS:

- 1 cup of flour
- 1/2 cup of quick oats
- 2 teaspoons of baking powder
- 1/4 cup of sugar
- 1/2 teaspoon of salt
- 1 large egg
- 1/4 cup of cannabis butter
- 1 cup of mil k
- 1 cup of fresh strawberries

DIRECTIONS:

1. Preheat oven to 380F-400F.

2. Mix together the oats, flour, baking powder, sugar and salt in a large mixing bowl.

3. In a smaller bowl, mix together the egg, milk and marijuana butter.

4. Make a crater in the large bowl, and then pour in the liquid mix from the smaller bowl.

5. Stir it up a little - don't stir until smooth - it should be lumpy.

6. Carefully insert the strawberries deep into the mix; you can slice the strawberries into halves and quarters if you wish.

7. Pour the mixture into a muffin tin, using muffin liners, make sure that you leave room in each muffin tin for them to rise. Your mix should fill about 75% of the capacity of the liners.

8. Bake for 25-30 minutes in an oven.

9. Leave to cool on a wire rack, and then enjoy!

ADULT WEED BROWNIES

INGREDIENTS:

- 1/4 pound butter
- 1/4 pound dark chocolate
- 1 cup of white sugar
- 4 regular eggs

- 1/2 cup plain flour
- Nutmeg
- Cinnamon
- 2 tablespoons of vanilla
- 1 ounce of finely ground cannabis bud (or 2-3 ounces of cannabis leaf, but is much better)

DIRECTIONS :

1. Preheat your oven to 350 degrees F.

2. Melt the butter over a low heat, then add the chocolate (in cubes is quickest) and melt that in with the already melted butter; stir regularly so that it becomes chocolate butter!

3. As soon as the chocolate has melted entirely, add the cinnamon, nutmeg and the white sugar; stir and simmer for a few minutes.

4. Add the eggs, one at a time, beating them so that the yolk breaks up. Continue to stir the mixture on a low heat until it is completely smooth.

5. Add the flour and finely ground cannabis to the mix. If you like nuts, then you can add a quarter of a cup of your favorite nut if you wish. Stir it well; if it is difficult to stir, then add a small dash of milk.

6. Pour your mixture into a greased 9x13 inch pan - if you don't have one then a smaller one is OK – it just means a thicker brownie and possibly a little longer in the oven.

7. Bake your mixture for 20-25 minutes, sometimes a little longer is required.

8. Once it looks and feels like a giant brownie, cut it into around 20 square. It doesn't matter how many squares, of course.

9. Dosage: Wait an hour and see how you feel. Then eat more as required! These brownies taste delicious and it is difficult to resist eating them, but you don't want to eat too many and then whitey!

HOT CANNA COCOA

Time: 25 minutes - **Serving Size:** 4 servings - **Prep Time:** 5 minutes - **Cook Time:** 20 minutes

INGREDIENTS:

- 6 ounces water
- 3 cups whole milk
- 3 tablespoons unsweetened cocoa powder
- 6 ounces finely chopped semi-sweet chocolate or semi-sweet chocolate chips
- 3 tablespoons sugar
- 1 teaspoon cannabis butter or a few drops of cannabis tincture

Equipment:

- Saucepan
- Whisk

* Mugs

DIRECTIONS:

1. Place the saucepan with the water in it over medium-high heat and let it come to a simmer.

2. Add the cocoa powder and whisk until smooth without lumps.

3. Whisk in the milk and bring the mixture back up to a simmer but not a boil.

4. Add in the sugar and chocolate and continue to whisk for a further five minutes, until the chocolate is completely melted and the whole mixture is creamy and smooth.

5. Pour the hot cocoa into the mugs and stir a teaspoon of cannabis butter into each mug. Alternatively, you can skip the butter and opt to add a few drops of cannabis tincture to your cocoa instead.

LEMONADE

Time: 1 hour 30 minutes - **Serving Size:** 8 servings - **Prep Time:** 3o minutes - **Cook Time:** 1 hour

INGREDIENTS:

* ½ cup of freshly squeezed lemon juice
* 3 ¼ cups water
* ¼ cup cranberry juice cocktail
* ⅔ cups of sugar
* 4 tablespoons cannabis tincture (Start with half the tincture to test the potency. You can add more as desired.)

Equipment:

* Saucepan
* Large airtight container

DIRECTIONS:

1. Place the saucepan with one cup of water in it over medium-high heat, then add the sugar to the saucepan. Dissolve the sugar by stirring and bring the mix up to a boil.

2. Once sugar is dissolved, allow the syrup to cool on a counter until it reaches room temperature. Transfer to an airtight container and refrigerate until chilled.

3. Combine the syrup and all the other ingredients in a large pitcher and serve your pink cannabis-infused lemonade chilled over ice cubes.

MARIJUANA MILKSHAKE

Time: 10 minutes - **Serving Size:** 1 serving - **Prep Time:** 5 minutes - **Cook Time**: 5 minutes

INGREDIENTS:

* 2 teaspoons cannabis tincture (Start with half the tincture or only a few drops and increase the dose as

desired.)

- 1 cup fresh or frozen strawberries
- 1 teaspoon vanilla extract
- 3/4 cup milk
- 1 cup strawberry ice cream

Equipment:

- Blender

DIRECTIONS:

1. Place all the ingredients into the blender and blend well until incorporated and the milkshake has a smooth consistency.
2. Pour into a mug or glass of your choice and enjoy.

THAI ICED TEA

Time: 15 minutes - **Serving Size:** 6 servings - **Prep Time**: 5 minutes - **Cook Time:** 10 minutes

INGREDIENTS:

- 6 chai tea bags (If you don't have chai tea, you can substitute 6 black tea bags and add in ½ teaspoon of ground cinnamon, one star anise pod, two cardamom pods, and ½ teaspoon vanilla extract.)
- 8 cups boiling water
- 1 14-ounce can condensed milk
- 3 to 5 tablespoons melted cannabis butter
- Optional: ¼ to ½ cup granulated sugar

Equipment:

- Large pitcher
- Small mixing bowl
- 6 glasses

DIRECTIONS:

1. Place your tea bags and spices in a large pitcher and pour in the boiling water. Allow the tea to steep for approximately four to five minutes before removing the tea bags and any whole spices.
2. Set the tea aside and allow it to cool down to room temperature.
3. While the tea is cooling, mix together the cannabutter and the condensed milk and set aside.
4. To serve, fill the six glasses with ice cubes, or half-fill them with crushed ice. Pour the tea into each glass, filling only two-thirds of a glass. Top it all off with two ounces of the condensed milk mixture. The condensed milk mix will sink to the bottom. Stir it all up and enjoy it.

THE PROPER PINEAPPLE SMOOTHIE

Time: 10 minutes - **Serving Size:** 2 servings - **Prep Time:** 5 minutes - **Cook Time**: 5 minutes

INGREDIENTS:

- 2 tablespoons cannabis-infused coconut oil
- 1 cup frozen sliced pineapple
- ¼ cup sliced banana
- ½ cup water
- ½ cup milk
- 1 teaspoon chia seeds (optional)

Equipment:

- Blender

DIRECTIONS:

1. Pack the banana and pineapple into the blender and pour in the water and milk. Blend the lot together until you have achieved a smooth consistency.
2. Gradually and slowly add the two tablespoons of canna coconut oil and blend until well incorporated.
3. Serve the pineapple smoothie in two glasses and top with chia seeds if you'd like.

MAYONNAISE

Time: 2 hours 10 minutes - **Serving Size**: 2 cups of canna mayo - **Prep Time:** 10 minutes - **Cook Time**: 2 hours

INGREDIENTS:

- 3 egg yolks
- 1 cup cannabis oil
- ½ teaspoon Dijon mustard
- 1 teaspoon white vinegar
- 1 teaspoon fresh lemon juice
- A pinch of sea salt

Equipment:

- 1 medium-sized bowl
- Whisk
- 1 appropriately-sized canning jar with a lid

DIRECTIONS:

1. In a medium-sized bowl, whisk together all of the ingredients, except the cannabis oil, until they are well incorporated.
2. Keep whisking and gradually pour the cannaoil into the mixture.
3. Whisk the lot until the mayonnaise starts to get thicker. If it becomes too thick, you can add a few drops

of water which will thin it out to your ideal consistency.

4. Pour the canna mayo into the canning jar and allow it to cool to room temperature before sealing and storing it in the fridge.

CAESAR SALAD DRESSING

Time: 20 minutes - **Serving Size**: 2 cups of salad dressing - **Prep Time:** 10 minutes - **Cook Time**: 10 minutes

INGREDIENTS:

- 1 ½ cups cannabis oil
- 2 eggs
- 10 cloves of garlic
- ½ cup lemon juice
- 2 teaspoons sea salt

Equipment:

- A small saucepan
- 1 canning jar with a lid

DIRECTIONS:

1. Pour the water into the saucepan and bring to a boil over medium to high heat.
2. Place the eggs in the water and boil them for 30 seconds. This pasteurizes the eggs.
3. Crack the eggs and combine in a blender with all the other ingredients except the cannaoil. Blend the concoction for approximately one minute.
4. Keep the blender switched on while slowly adding the cannabis oil to the mixture until everything is well blended.
5. Pour the salad dressing into the jar, seal, and store in the fridge.
6. Give the jar a good shake before serving to mix any ingredients that may have sunken to the bottom of the jar.

LEMON VINAIGRETTE

Time: 15 minutes - **Serving Size:** Approximately 1 ¼ cups of vinaigrette - **Prep Time:** 10 minutes - **Cook Time**: 5 minutes

INGREDIENTS:

- ¼ cup cannabis olive oil
- ¾ cup extra-virgin olive oil
- ¼ cup fresh lemon juice

- ¼ teaspoon honey
- 1 teaspoon minced garlic
- 1 teaspoon dried oregano

Equipment:

- Blender
- 1 bottle or canning jar with a lid

DIRECTIONS:

1. Throw all of the ingredients to your blender, switch it on, and blend until everything is well incorporated. That's it – super simple and easy-to-make vinaigrette.
2. Pour the cannabis-infused vinaigrette into a bottle or jar and store it in the fridge.
3. Give the vinaigrette a good shake before use to mix up any ingredients that may have sunken to the bottom.

BBQ SAUCE

Time: 3 hours 10 minutes **- Serving Size**: 2 cups of sauce **- Prep Time:** 10 minutes **- Cook Time**: 3 hours

INGREDIENTS:

- ⅓ ounce of average decarboxylated cannabis
- ⅓ cup vegetable oil
- Juice of 1 lime
- 2 tablespoons Worcestershire sauce
- 2 tablespoons apple cider vinegar
- 1 tablespoons soy sauce
- ¾ tomato paste
- 1 tablespoon honey
- ½ cup apricot nectar
- ¼ cup water
- 2 tablespoons dark brown sugar
- 1 tablespoon fresh minced garlic
- 3 tablespoons of chopped green onion
- ½ tablespoons chili powder
- A pinch of cayenne pepper
- A pinch of ground ginger

Equipment:

- A crockpot
- 1 canning jar with a lid

DIRECTIONS:

1. Finely crumble the cannabis and put it in a crockpot, along with the water and lime juice. Cook for around two hours.
2. Add the rest of the ingredients to the crockpot and mix well until everything is incorporated.
3. Cook for an additional hour, stirring regularly.
4. Pour your cannabis BBQ sauce into the canning jar and allow it to cool to room temperature before sealing. Store your sauce in the fridge and give it a shake before use so that any ingredients that sink to the bottom get mixed up again.

PESTO

Time: 15 minutes - **Serving Size:** Approximately 1 cup of pesto - **Prep Time:** 10 minutes - **Cook Time**: 5 minutes

INGREDIENTS:

- Walnuts
- ¼ cup freshly grated Parmesan cheese
- 1 cup cannabis-infused olive oil
- 2 cloves garlic
- 2 cups basil
- A pinch of sea salt

Equipment:

- 1 canning jar with a lid
- Blender
- Saucepan

DIRECTIONS:

1. Use medium heat to warm up a skillet and toast the pine nuts. This will take approximately three minutes. Keep stirring the nuts to prevent them from burning.
2. Take the saucepan off the heat and let the pine nuts cool down.
3. Put the pine nuts in your blender and blend on high until they are ground up to resemble a coarse flour.
4. Rinse the basil off and pat dry with a paper towel before removing the stems and breaking the leaves into small pieces.
5. Add all of the remaining ingredients except the cannaoil to the ground pine nuts in the blender.
6. Switch the processor on medium to low speed and, while it's blending the ingredients, gradually add 1/3 of the cup of cannaoil. Add the basil, garlic, salt, and Parmesan to the walnut flour in the food processor.
7. Taste the pesto and add more salt or cannaoil until the taste and consistency is to your liking.

SRIRACHA HOT SAUCE

Time: 24 hours **- Serving Size**: Approximately 1 cup of sriracha sauce **- Prep Time:** 10 minutes **- Cook Time**: 24 hours

INGREDIENTS:

- ½ cup cannabis cooking oil
- 8 cloves of garlic
- 12 hot chili peppers of your choice (The hotter the peppers, the hotter your siracha will be.)
- ¼ cup apple cider vinegar
- 3 tablespoons of honey (You can use cannabis-infused honey for an extra kick if you like.)

Equipment:

- Aluminum foil
- A baking sheet
- A blender/food processor
- 1 canning jar with a lid

DIRECTIONS:

1. Switch your oven on and preheat it to 350° F.
2. Cover the baking sheet with aluminum foil so that every inch of it is covered.
3. Lay the chili peppers on the foil-covered sheet and roast them for 10 minutes.
4. Remove the sheet from the oven and rotate the peppers.
5. Spread the garlic evenly on the baking sheet and return it to the oven to bake for a further 10 minutes.
6. Remove the baking sheet from the oven and allow the peppers and garlic to cool until you can handle them without burning your fingers. Remove the stems from the chili peppers.
7. Put the peppers and garlic into the food processor along with the rest of the ingredients. You can also always add some more garlic if you like a lot of garlic.
8. Turn that blender on and keep going until everything is blended together and your sriracha sauce has a smooth consistency. If you like it a bit chunkier, simply blend until the sauce reaches your desired chunkiness.
9. Pour the sauce into the canning jar and allow it to cool completely.
10. Seal the jar and store in the fridge. Allow your sriracha sauce to sit for 24 hours before you use it so that all the flavors meld together.

GUACAMOLE

Time: 25 minutes **- Serving Size:** Serves 2 **- Prep Time:** 10 minutes **- Cook Time**: 15 minutes
INGREDIENTS:

- 1 avocado
- Juice of ⅓ lime
- ⅓ teaspoon salt (or to taste)
- ¼ cup diced onion
- 1 tablespoons fresh cilantro
- ¾ teaspoons carboxylated cannabis
- ¾ plum or Roma tomatoes
- ⅓ teaspoon minced garlic
- ⅓ teaspoon cannabis oil
- A pinch of ground cayenne pepper

Equipment:

- A medium-sized mixing bowl

DIRECTIONS:

1. Grind up the cannabis until it's fine, dice the tomatoes, and chop up the cilantro.
2. Peel, remove the pits, and smash up the avocados. You can leave the smashed avocados slightly chunky or you can use a blender to achieve a smooth consistency.
3. Put all of the ingredients into the bowl and mix it all up until it's well combined.

SPICED NUTS

Time: 40 minutes plus cooling time - **Serving Size:** 3 cups of spicy nuts - **Prep Time:** 10 minutes - **Cook Time**: 30 minutes

INGREDIENTS:

- 1 cup pecans
- 1 cup walnuts
- 1 cup cashews
- 1 teaspoon ground cumin
- 2 tablespoons curry powder
- Pinch of cayenne
- ½ teaspoon ground cardamom
- Salt to taste
- 3 tablespoons of cannabis oil

Equipment:

- Baking sheet
- Mixing bowl
- Non-stick cooking spray

DIRECTIONS:

1. Start off by switching your oven on to 300° F to preheat while you prepare the nuts.
2. Spray a baking sheet or two with non-stick spray and set aside.
3. Toss all the ingredients in a large mixing bowl, ensuring that all ingredients are well mixed and that all the nuts are evenly and well coated.
4. Spread out the coated nuts on one or two baking sheets. Don't overcrowd the baking sheet – spread the nuts out evenly, allowing spaces between them for a better result.
5. Bake them for 20 to 30 minutes, stirring them up and around regularly to turn and toast them evenly.
6. After baking, remove from the oven, let cool, and store in an airtight container.

SPICY CHICKPEAS

Time: 40 minutes plus cooling time - **Serving Size:** 16 ounces of spiced chickpeas - **Prep Time:** 10 minutes - **Cook Time**: 30 minutes

INGREDIENTS:

- 1 16-ounce can chickpeas
- 2 tablespoon cannabis olive oil
- ¼ teaspoon ground cumin
- ¼ teaspoon ground ginger
- ¼ teaspoon paprika (smoked is preferable, but plain will do just fine)
- ¼ teaspoon salt

Equipment:

- Colander or strainer
- Large mixing bowl
- Baking sheet
- Non-stick cooking spray or parchment paper

DIRECTIONS:

1. Before you prepare the chickpeas, set your oven to 375° F so that it can preheat.
2. Drain the chickpeas in a colander or strainer.
3. Using a large mixing bowl, mix together all the ingredients until the chickpeas are well and evenly coated.
4. Spray a baking sheet with non-stick spray or line it with parchment paper to prevent sticking.
5. Spread the coated nuts out on the baking sheet evenly and bake for 30 minutes or until the chickpeas start to crisp.
6. Allow to cool and store in an airtight container.

SAVORY POPCORN

Time: 15 minutes plus cooling time - **Serving Size:** 1 serving - **Prep Time:** 5 minutes - **Cook Time:** 10 minutes

INGREDIENTS:

- 1/4 cup cannabis-infused butter
- 1/2 cup popcorn kernels
- 1/4 cup canola/vegetable oil
- Salt to taste

Equipment:

Large stockpot with a lid

DIRECTIONS:

1. Over medium-high heat, warm oil in a large stockpot.
2. Drop two to three corn kernels in the oil and cover the pot. When the oil is hot enough, the kernels will pop. When the test kernels pop, add the rest of the corn kernels, spreading them evenly across the bottom of the pot.
3. Cover the pot and let the kernels pop.
4. Shake the pot gently to shift the kernels so that all of them have a chance to pop.
5. Popping should occur in rapid succession. When the popping slows to two or so seconds between pops, it's time to remove the pot from the heat.
6. Drop the cannabis butter into the pot and mix well to evenly coat the popcorn. Sprinkle with salt as desired.

POTATO CHIPS

Time: 25 minutes - **Serving Size:** 2 servings - **Prep Time:** 10 minutes - **Cook Time:** 15 minutes

INGREDIENTS:

- ¼ cup of cannabis cooking oil
- 1 large potato
- 1 tablespoon salt or 1 tablespoon popcorn seasoning of your choice

Equipment:

- Large baking sheet
- Parchment paper
- Vegetable peeler
- Knife

DIRECTIONS:

1. Set your oven temperature to 400° F and let it heat up while you prepare your potato chips.

2. Line the baking sheet with parchment paper to prevent your chips from sticking.

3. Peel the potato and slice it as thinly as possible into chips. Using a vegetable peeler to slice the chips is effective for achieving thin slices that will crisp well in the oven.

4. Spread out the potato chip slices evenly on your lined baking sheet and drizzle them with the cannabis oil infusion. Coat each chip evenly and well.

5. Place the baking sheet in the center of the preheated oven and bake for about 15 minutes or until golden brown and crispy.

6. Remove the baking sheet from the oven, sprinkle your salt or seasoning over them evenly to taste, and allow the potato chips to cool for about 5 minutes.

BUFFALO CHEX MIX

Time: 55 minutes - **Serving Size:** 3 cups of buffalo Chex mix (serving size suggestion: ¾ cup of mix) - **Prep Time:** 10 minutes - **Cook Time**: 45 minutes

INGREDIENTS:

- ¾ cup Rice Chex cereal
- ¾ cup Corn Chex cereal
- ½ cup rye chips
- ¼ cup of peanuts
- ½ cup small cheddar cheese crackers such as Cheez-Its
- ½ cup pretzels
- ¾ tablespoon cannabis butter
- ¼ tablespoon regular butter
- 1 ounce buffalo sauce
- ¼ packet of dry powdered ranch dressing mix

Equipment:

- Large mixing bowl
- Medium saucepan
- Large baking sheet
- Parchment paper (optional)
- Non-stick cooking spray (optional)

DIRECTIONS:

1. Switch your oven on to 250° F and allow it to preheat while you prepare the mix for baking.

2. Spray a large baking sheet with non-stick cooking spray or, alternatively, line it with a piece of parchment paper and set it aside.

3. In a large mixing bowl, toss the peanuts, crackers, pretzels, both types of Chex cereal, and rye chips and set aside.

4. Set a medium saucepan over medium heat and melt the cannabis butter and regular butter together. Once the butters are melted and combined, mix in the buffalo sauce.

5. Pour the butter and buffalo sauce mixture over the dry ingredients in the mixing bowl and toss well to thoroughly and evenly coat the ingredients.

6. Pour the Chex mix onto your prepared baking sheet, spreading it out evenly in a single layer, and sprinkle the dry ranch dressing over the mix.

7. Place the baking sheet in the center of the oven and bake for 45 minutes. Stir the mix every 15 minutes to prevent clumping and ensure an even bake.

8. Once baked, remove the baking sheet from the oven and place on a countertop to cool. Allow to cool completely and store the buffalo Chex mix in an airtight container for up to one week.

BAKED KALE CHIPS

Time: 20 minutes plus cooling time - **Serving Size:** 2 servings of kale chips - **Prep Time**: 10 minutes - **Cook Time**: 10 minutes

INGREDIENTS:

- 1/2 bunch of kale
- 1/2 tablespoon of cannabis butter
- Salt to taste or seasoning spices of your choice

Equipment:

- Baking sheet
- Parchment paper
- Heat-proof ramekin

DIRECTIONS:

1. Preheat your oven by setting the temperature to 375° F and ensure that the oven rack is placed in the center.

2. Line the baking sheet with a piece of parchment paper and set it aside.

3. Wash and thoroughly dry the kale leaves. Remove the stalk from each leaf and then tear each leaf into pieces. The leaf pieces should be around twice the size of a regular tortilla chip. Don't worry if this seems like it's a bit big, the kale chips will shrink in size as they bake so you want to make the raw chips bigger than you want the final baked chips to be.

4. Place the kale chips on the lined baking tray, spreading them out as evenly as possible and ensuring that they form only one layer with no overlapping.

5. Melt the cannabis butter in the ramekin using a microwave. This will only take a few seconds. Alternatively, you can place the ramekin in the preheating oven to melt the butter.

6. Drizzle the melted cannabutter over your spread-out kale leaves. If the coverage isn't sufficient, add some extra regular butter or some olive oil.

7. To ensure even coverage and a better finished kale chip, massage the drizzled butter into each piece of kale leaf. However, you can skip this step if it seems like too much work.

8. Sprinkle the kale with salt or seasoning spices of your choice.

9. Place the baking sheet into the oven and bake the kale for roughly 8 to 10 minutes or until the chips are browned but have not burned.

10. Once baked, remove the baking sheet from the oven and set aside on a countertop to cool off. The kale chips will become crispier as they cool.

11. Store any leftover kale chips in a single layer and cover loosely. Contrary to storage instructions for many other snack foods, don't store your leftovers in an airtight container, as this will cause them to lose their crisp.

HUSH PUPPIES

Time: 45 minutes - **Serving Size**: Dependent on the size of batter dollops - **Prep Time:** 15 minutes - **Cook Time**: 30 minutes

INGREDIENTS:

- 6 cups of your preferred regular cooking oil
- 1 cup of cannabis milk
- 1 ½ cups of self-rising cornmeal
- ½ teaspoon salt
- ½ cup self-rising flour, all-purpose
- ½ teaspoon baking soda
- 1 beaten egg

Equipment:

- Deep fryer
- Mixing bowls
- Teaspoon

DIRECTIONS:

1. Switch the deep fryer on and add the cooking oil, allowing it to heat up to 350° F.

2. Combine the dry ingredients in a mixing bowl and mix well.

3. Using a second mixing bowl, combine the cannabis milk and egg, mixing until incorporated.

4. Add the wet ingredients to the bowl with the dry ingredients and mix thoroughly.

5. Use a teaspoon to scoop out batter and drop it into the hot oil in small dollops. Fry the dollops of batter, turning once, until each side is a rich golden brown color.

6. Be careful not to overcrowd the fryer or to burn the hush puppies. Frying smaller batches at a time offers you better control over the cooking process.

7. Fry all of the batter until finished.

8. Remove each batch of fried hush puppies and lay them between two layers of paper town to absorb any excess oil.

9. Serve warm and enjoy.

NO-BAKE CANNABIS COOKIE BARS

INGREDIENTS:

- 1/2 cup melted cannabis butter
- 1 1/2 cups Graham cracker crumbs
- One pound confectioners' sugar (3 to 3 1/2 cups)
- 1 1/2 cups peanut butter
- 1/2 cup butter, melted
- 1 (12 ounces) bag milk chocolate chips

DIRECTIONS:

1. Combine Graham cracker crumbs, sugar and peanut butter; mix well.
2. Blend in the melted cannabis butter until well combined .
3. Press mixture evenly into a 9 x 13-inch pan.
4. Melt chocolate chips in microwave or in a double boiler.
5. Spread over peanut butter mixture.
6. Chill until just set and cut into bars. (These are very hard to cut if the chocolate gets "rock hard"

CHOCOLATE BANANAS

INGREDIENTS:

- ½ cup cannabutter
- 3 ripe but firm bananas
- 1 pound dark chocolate, chopped, or semisweet chocolate chips
- 1/2 cup granola, chopped pecans and walnuts, or sprinkles (optional)

DIRECTIONS :

1. Line a baking sheet with nonstick foil or parchment paper.
2. Cut the bananas in half and insert a popsicle stick into each half, as shown.
3. Place them on the baking sheet and freeze for 15 minutes.
4. Melt the cannabutter over a low heat and then set it aside.

5. Melt chocolate in the same double boiler until smooth. Add the cannabutter to the chocolate as it's melting. Gently mix the cannabutter into the chocolate.

6. Roll each banana half in the chocolate, then quickly sprinkle with your topping (if using).

7. Freeze until the chocolate sets, 30 minutes.

8. Serve and then enjoy! Or freeze in an airtight container for up to a week.

CREAMY STUFFED CANNABIS-INFUSED PANCAKES

INGREDIENTS:

- 1 cup cannabis milk
- 1 egg
- 2 tablespoons vegetable oil
- 1 teaspoon salt
- 2 tablespoons sugar
- 1 cup flour
- 2 teaspoons baking powder (for the filling)
- 1 cup cream cheese
- Chopped strawberries
- Blueberries
- 2 tablespoons vanilla sugar
- 1/2 cup whipping cream

DIRECTIONS :

1. In a large bowl, sift together the flour, baking powder, salt, and sugar. Make a well in the center and pour in the milk, egg and vegetable oil; mix until smooth.

2. Heat a lightly oiled griddle or frying pan over medium-high to low heat. Pour or scoop the batter onto the griddle. Brown on both sides and serve hot.

For Filling:

1. In a medium mixing bowl, beat the softened cream cheese until smooth.

2. Add whipping cream and vanilla. Beat mixture until combined. Stir in both berries and sugar.

3. To serve, spoon 2/3 tablespoons of filling onto each thin pancake.

4. Serve with chocolate sauce.

CHOCOLATE WEED BROWNIES

INGREDIENTS:

- 1/4 cup cannabis butter
- 1/4 cup normal butter
- 2 eggs
- 1 teaspoon vanilla extract
- 1/3 cup unsweetened cocoa powder
- 1/2 cup all-purpose flour
- 1/4 teaspoon salt
- 1/4 teaspoon baking powder

For the Frosting:

- 3 tablespoons butter, softened
- 1 teaspoon cannabis butter, softened
- 1 tablespoon honey
- 1 teaspoon vanilla extrac t
- 1 cup confectioners' sugar

DIRECTIONS:

1. Preheat oven to 330 degrees F.

2. Grease and flour an 8-inch square pan.

3. In a large saucepan, on very low heat, melt 1/4 cup butter and 1/4 cup cannabis butter. Remove from heat, and stir in sugar, eggs and 1 teaspoon vanilla. Beat in 1/3 cup cocoa, 1/2 cup flour, salt and baking powder. Spread batter into prepared pan.

4. Bake in preheated oven for 25 to 30 minutes. Do not overcook.

For the Frosting:

1. Combine 3 tablespoons softened butter and 1 teaspoon cannabis butter; add 3 tablespoons cocoa, honey, 1 teaspoon vanilla extract, and 1 cup confectioners' sugar. Stir until smooth.

2. Frost brownies while they are still warm.

HOW TO MAKE WEED CANDY

INGREDIENTS:

- 2 cups sugar
- 1¼ cup cannabis corn syrup
- 1 cup water
- Food coloring/flavoring of your choice

DIRECTIONS:

1. Heat sugar, cannabis corn syrup and water in saucepan over medium heat.

2. Stir until all sugars are dissolved. Bring to a 300 degree boil.

3. Add food coloring and flavoring slowly. Stir well.

4. Turn off heat. Carefully and quickly pour liquid into candy molds before it hardens.

5. Remove candy from mold once it is finished cooling. Toss candy in sugar, if desired.

CANNABIS CARAMEL CANDY

INGREDIENTS:

- 1 cup cannabutter
- 2 ¼ cups brown sugar
- Dash salt
- 1 cup light corn syrup
- 14 ounces sweetened condensed milk (canned)
- 1 teaspoon vanilla extract

DIRECTIONS:

1. Melt cannabutter slowly in saucepan .

2. Stir in brown sugar and salt until combined.

3. Stir in light corn syrup.

4. Add milk slowly while constantly stirring.

5. Cook mixture over medium heat until candy begins to get firmer (usually 12 to 15 minutes).

6. Remove saucepan from heat and stir in the vanilla extract.

7. Pour mixture into 9x13 pan. Allow candy to cool down.

8. Cut, serve and store.

CARAMEL CASHEW SQUARES

INGREDIENTS:

For Crust:

- 1/3 cup firmly packed brown sugar
- 4 tablespoons butter (2 cannabutter, 2 regular)
- 1 cup all-purpose flour
- 1/4 teaspoon sal t

For Topping:

- 1/2 cup butterscotch-flavored baking chips
- 1/4 cup light corn syrup
- 2 tablespoons cannabutter

- 1 cup chopped salted cashews

DIRECTIONS:

1. Heat oven to 350°F.

2. Place brown sugar in medium bowl.

3. Add 4 tablespoons of butter, and mix with brown sugar in a blender until it resembles coarse crumbs.

4. Add flour and salt. Mix well.

5. Press mixture onto bottom of the ungreased 8-inch square baking pan.

6. Bake for 11-13 minutes and let set.

7. Melt butterscotch chips, corn syrup and 2 tablespoons cannabutter in 2-quart saucepan over low heat, stirring occasionally.

8. Remove from heat. Stir in cashews.

9. Pour cashew mixture over the crust.

10. Continue baking for 8-10 minutes or until it starts to bubble. Set and cool completely.

11. Cover; store refrigerated. Cut into bars.

HOMEMADE CANNABIS OREO COOKIES

INGREDIENTS:

- 1 cup 50/50 butter/cannabis butter mixed
- 1 cup sugar
- 2 teaspoons salt
- 2 large eggs
- 2 cups all-purpose flour
- 1 ¼ cups dark cocoa powder
- ½ teaspoon baking soda

For Cream Filling:

- ½ cup cannabis butter
- 2 cups powdered sugar
- 1 teaspoon vanilla

DIRECTIONS :

1. Preheat oven to 325 degrees F .

2. In a large bowl, cream together 1/2 cup cannabis butter with ½ cup normal butter. Mix with the white sugar and salt until light and fluffy.

3. Beat in eggs until fully incorporated.

4. Sieve together the flour, cocoa powder, and baking soda into the mix. Blend well.

5. Add the dry ingredients to the wet ingredients, and mix together until combined.

6. Turn the dough out onto your surface and push together into a flat square. Wrap the dough in plastic wrap and refrigerate for 1 hour.

For Cream Filling:

1. To make the filling, combine ½ cup cannabis butter, powdered sugar, and vanilla in a medium mixing bowl. Beat together until light and fluffy.

2. Remove the dough from the fridge, and for ease of rolling out, divide the dough into 4 pieces.

3. To roll out the dough, place a quarter of the dough between two sheets of parchment paper. Roll the dough between the two sheets of parchment to ¼-inch thickness .

4. Using a small round cookie cutter or champagne glass, cut the dough into individual rounds and place on a large parchment-lined baking sheet, leaving at least ½-inch between each cookie.

5. Pack together and re-roll out any scraps to cut additional cookies. Repeat this process with each remaining ¼ of the dough.

6. Bake in preheated oven for 15 minutes.

7. Remove and transfer cookies to a cooling rack to cool completely.

8. Assemble the cookies by spreading a generous scoop of the icing onto one of the cookies and sandwiching it with another. Give it a light squeeze and scrape any excess off to clear and even out the sides.

9. Serve with a glass of milk.

CANNABIS CHOCOLATE ICE CREAM WITH SUPER POTENT BLONDIES

INGREDIENTS:

- 4 tablespoons cannabis butter
- 1 can condensed milk
- 1 teaspoon vanilla extract
- 1/2 cup cocoa powder
- 2 cups heavy cream
- 1/2 cup cannabis butter
- 1 cup light brown suga r
- 1 egg
- 1 teaspoon vanilla extract
- 1 cup flour
- 1/2 teaspoon baking powder

- 1/8 teaspoon baking soda
- Pinch of salt
- 1 cup white chocolate

DIRECTIONS:

1. Preheat oven to 220 degrees F.

2. In a medium bowl, mix your condensed milk, 4 tablespoons cannabis butter, vanilla and cocoa powder; set aside.

3. In another bowl, whip your whipping cream until stiff.

4. Fold your chocolate mixture into your whipping cream mixture using a spatula.

5. Freeze for at least 6 hours

6. In a medium bowl, mix together your cannabis butter with brown sugar using an electric hand mixer.

7. Add your egg and vanilla and mix again.

8. Now add your flour, baking powder, baking soda and salt; mix again.

9. Fold in your white chocolate using a spatula.

 Place your mixture on a floured baking tray and bake for 40 minutes.

10. Serve little chunks on your chocolate ice cream.

CANNABIS CHOCOLATE CARAMEL PEANUT BUTTER CUPS

INGREDIENTS:

- 4 tablespoons cannabis butter
- 2 1/2 cups chocolate
- 1/2 cup salted caramel sauce
- 1 cup peanut butte r
- 1/2 cup powdered sugar
- 1/4 cup cornflakes
- Pinch of salt

DIRECTIONS:

1. Take a medium bowl and melt chocolate au bain marie with your cannabis butter.

2. Mix using a spatula so your cannabis butter is evenly mixed into the chocolate.

3. Put your chocolate cannabis mix in a piping bag and let cool slightly.

4. Line up a tray with 12 paper cupcake cups.

5. Use half of your chocolate cannabis mix to fill out the cups evenly. A thin layer just so the bottom is covered will do.

6. Freeze for 5 minutes until chocolate is solid.

7. Add a good tablespoon of caramel sauce to each chocolate cup.

8. Freeze again for 5 minutes

9. In a medium small bowl, mix 1 cup peanut butter with the cornflakes, powdered sugar and cannabis butter using a hand mixer.

10. Add a full tablespoon of peanut butter to your chocolate cups.

11. Now use the other half of your cannabis chocolate to cover the peanut butter.

12. Freeze for about 15 - 20 minutes.

13. Serve.

POTENT CANNABIS BROWNIES

INGREDIENTS:

- 1 cup cannabis butter
- 2/3 cup chocolate
- 1 teaspoon vanilla extract
- Orange zest (optional)
- 5 egg whites
- 4 egg yolk s
- 3/4 cup sugar
- 1/3 cup flour
- 1 tablespoon cocoa powder
- 1/2 cup crushed pecan nuts

DIRECTIONS:

1. Preheat oven to 220 degrees F.

2. Use a double boiler by placing a bowl on top of a pot with water over medium high heat.

3. Add your chocolate, cannabis butter, vanilla extract and orange zest to the empty bowl and mix to incorporate.

4. Take the bowl off the heat and set aside. (You will not need any heat anymore from this point on.)

5. Place your egg whites in a separate bowl.

6. Beat egg whites until you form stiff white peaks, using an electric mixer or a whisk; set aside.

7. Add your egg yolks to another separate bowl and add sugar. Mix to incorporate.

8. Add your chocolate cannabis mixture to the egg-yolk mixture and slowly incorporate both using a spatula.

9. Once incorporated, sift in your flour, cocoa powder and add your pecan nuts.

10. Now add your fluffy white egg whites to the mixture, and incorporate everything together using a spatula .

11. Line a baking pan with parchment paper and add your finished mixture to it.

12. Now bake for 60 minutes, and your brownies will be ready.

CANNABIS-INFUSED ICE CREAM

INGREDIENTS:

- 4 tablespoons cannabis butter
- 2 cups whipping cream
- 1 can (14oz) condensed milk
- 1/2 teaspoon vanilla extract
- 1/4 cup chopped mint

DIRECTIONS:

1. Whip the cream until stiff; add all remaining ingredients in separate bowl and mix.

2. Now fold the mixture into the whipping cream. Store in a container and freeze for 6 hours.

3. Serve the cannabis Ice cream.

WEED BANANA BREAD

INGREDIENTS:

- 2 cups flour
- 1/2 cup sugar
- 1 teaspoon baking soda
- 1/2 teaspoon salt
- 1 1/2 cups mashed ripe bananas
- 1/4 cup honey or agave nectar (lower glycemic index)
- 1/4 cup sour cream
- 2 large eggs, lightly beaten
- 6 tablespoons melted butter
- 1 teaspoon vanilla
- 1 1/4 cups toasted and chopped pecans

DIRECTIONS:

1. Preheat oven to 350 degrees F. Grease and flour a 9X5 inch loaf pan and set aside.

2. In a medium bowl, combine the flour, sugar, baking soda and salt; then, mix well and set aside. In a large bowl, mix the mashed bananas, honey, sour cream, eggs, melted butter and vanilla.

3. Lightly fold the dry ingredients into the wet ingredients, mixing only until incorporated. Stir in the chopped pecans. Batter will be lumpy.

4. Pour batter into prepared pan and bake for 50-60 minutes, or until a tester comes out clean.

5. Cool in pan for 5 minutes, then transfer to a wire rack to cool completely.

OMFG MINT CANNABIS BROWNIES

INGREDIENTS:

- 1 cup cannabutter
- 6 ounces unsweetened chocolate
- 2 cups sugar
- 1 teaspoon baking powder
- 1½ teaspoons vanilla
- ½ teaspoon salt
- 1½ cups flou r
- 1 cup walnuts or pecans, finely ground
- 1 1/2 ounces bag Hershey's mint chocolate chips
- 4 eggs

DIRECTIONS:

1. Preheat oven to

2. In a medium saucepan, melt cannabutter and unsweetened chocolate over low heat, stirring constantly. Remove from heat and let cool.

3. Grease 9×13 inch pan and set aside. Stir sugar into cooled chocolate mixture in saucepan. Beat eggs, and add slowly to chocolate mixture. Stir in vanilla.

4. In a bowl, stir together the flour, baking soda and salt.

5. Add flour mixture to chocolate mixture until combined. Stir in nuts and mint chocolate chips. Spread the batter in the prepared pan.

6. Bake for 30 minutes. Cool on wire rack before storing.

POPPY-POT CAKE

INGREDIENTS:

For Cake :

- 1 3/4 cups cannaflour
- 1/2 teaspoon baking powder
- 1/2 teaspoon baking soda
- 1/8 teaspoon salt

- 1/2 cup unsalted cannabutter, softened
- 1 1/4 cups sugar
- 3 eggs
- 1 cup creme fraiche
- 3 tablespoons poppy seeds
- 1/2 teaspoon almond extract

For Frosting:

- 4 ounces cream cheese, softened
- 2/3 cup powdered suga r
- 1 cup creme fraiche
- 1 teaspoon finely grated lemon peel
- 1/8 teaspoon almond extract

DIRECTIONS:

1. Preheat oven to 350 degrees F. Spray bottom of a 9-inch square pan with nonstick cooking spray.

2. In a medium bowl, stir together cannaflour, baking powder, baking soda and salt.

3. In a large bowl, beat butter at a medium speed for 30 seconds, until creamy. Add sugar, beat for 5 minutes or until light, creamy and fluffy. Add eggs one at a time, beating until blended.

4. At low speed, beat in flour mixture in 3 parts alternately, with 1 cup creme fraiche, beginning and ending with flour mixture. Beat in poppy seeds and 1/2 teaspoon almond extract.

5. Spoon and spread batter into pan (It will be very thick). Bake 35-40 minutes or until dark golden brown and toothpick inserted in center comes out clean. Cool completely on wire rack.

6. Right before serving, in another large bowl, beat cream cheese and powdered sugar at low speed until smooth. Slowly beat in 1 cup creme fraiche until blended. Increase speed to medium; beat frosting until firm, but do not let stiff peaks form. Beat in lemon peel and 1/8 teaspoon almond extract.

7. Spread frosting over cake. Store in refrigerator.

PURPLE KUSH CAKE

INGREDIENTS:

- ¾ cup THC oil1
- 25 ounce Betty Crocker Super Moist Dark Chocolate Mix
- 3 eggs
- 2 cups cold milk
- One 16-ounce tub Betty Crocker Rich & Creamy Vanilla Frosting

DIRECTIONS:

1. Preheat oven to 400 degrees F.

2. Mix together the cake referencing the package directions. Use the infused oil instead of cooking oil and mix it with the eggs and water.

3. Pour the cake mixture into 2 evenly sized pans, and bake for 30 minutes or until a knife comes out of the cake clean.

4. Mix the frosting until smooth and spread a layer over the top of one cake. Put the other cake on top to create a cake sandwich. Now smother the entire cake in frosting and enjoy!

CANNA COFFEE AND TEA

Coffee has become a mighty industry, with popular brands and outlets each offering that something special to get you hooked and keep you coming back for more. You can be your own brewmaster right at home by adding a canna-caffeine boost to your favorite coffee. Three simple ways of making cannabis-infused coffee include:

- Adding cannabis-infused milk instead of regular milk
- Adding a cannabis tincture to your cup
- Using cannabis-infused sugar in place of regular sugar

Time: 10 minutes - **Serving Size:** 1 cup of coffee - **Prep Time**: 5 minutes - **Cook Time**: 5 minutes

INGREDIENTS:

- 1 cup of coffee or tea, slightly cooled
- Canna milk/sugar/tincture

DIRECTIONS:

Making a basic cup of cannabis coffee or tea is really simple. You just brew your tea or coffee as usual and either add a few drops of the tincture to your cup or replace your regular milk or sugar with the cannabis-infused version. We have easy recipes to follow in Chapter 2 that will guide you through making your own cannabis infusions for your edibles.

ICED CANNA COFFEE

Time: 5 minutes - **Serving Size:** 1 to 2 servings - **Prep Time:** 2 minutes - **Cook Time**: 3 minutes

INGREDIENTS:

- 1/2 cup warm water
- 5 ounces sweetened condensed milk
- 2 teaspoons instant coffee granules
- 1/2 cup cannabis-infused milk
- 1 tablespoon chocolate syrup
- 12 ice cubes

Equipment:

- Blender
- Small bowl

DIRECTIONS:

1. In a small bowl, dissolve the coffee in the water.
2. Pour the coffee into the blender and add all the other ingredients. Flip the 'on' switch and blend until your iced coffee has the ideal consistency.

Tip: You can keep some of the ice cubes aside and add them to the cup before pouring in the iced coffee.

Note: If you don't normally have cannabis milk at hand, you can substitute regular milk and add your canna kick in the form of a few drops of tincture instead.

CHOCOLATE OLIVE OIL CAKE

Preparation Time: 15 minutes- **Cooking Time:** 30 minutes - **Servings**: 6-8

INGREDIENTS:

- 3 cups all-purpose flour
- 2 cups of sugar
- 6 tablespoons good-quality cocoa powder
- 2 teaspoons baking soda
- 1 teaspoon salt
- ½ cup finely chopped nuts or dried fruit (optional)
- ¾ cup canna oil
- 2 tablespoons white vinegar
- 1 tablespoon vanilla
- 2 cups cold water Powdered sugar, for dusting

DIRECTIONS:

1. Preheat the oven to 350°F. Grease and flour two 8-inch cake pans or lines a 12-cup muffin tin with muffin liners. In a bowl, put in sugar and flour, cocoa powder, baking soda, salt, and nuts or dried fruit (if using). Whisk to incorporate. In another bowl, whisk together the oil, vinegar, vanilla, and water, then add to the flour mixture. With a hand mixer on medium-low speed, mix just until smooth. Pour into the prepared cake pans or muffin tin. Bake 30 to 40 minutes for cake or 20 to 25 minutes for muffins, or until a toothpick inserted in the center comes out clean (start checking early to avoid over baking). Cool completely. Before serving, dust with powdered sugar.

Nutrition:

Calories: 210, Fat: 6.8g, Fiber: 4.1, Carbs: 34.6g, Protein: 2.1g

ORANGE ALMOND CAKE

Preparation Time: 15 minutes- **Cooking Time:** 45-50 minutes - **Servings:** 6-8

INGREDIENTS:

- 2 cups packed almond flour, plus more for dusting
- 1 teaspoon baking powder
- ½ teaspoon baking soda
- 1 teaspoon ground cinnamon
- 1 teaspoon ground ginger
- ½ teaspoon salt
- 3 eggs, lightly beaten⅔ cup honey plus1 teaspoon, divided
- ¼ cup canna oil
- Zest and juice (¼ cup) of 1 orange
- 1 cup fresh raspberries

DIRECTIONS:

1. Preheat the oven to 325°F. Grease a 9-inch spring form pan and dust the inside with almond flour. In a large bowl, whisk together the almond flour, baking powder, baking soda, cinnamon, ginger, and salt. In another bowl, whisk together the eggs, ⅔ cup of the honey, oil, and orange zest. The dry ingredients will then be added to the egg mixture and fold in until just a few lumps remain, then gently fold in the raspberries. Put the mixture in the prepared pan and smoothen the top part. Bake for 45 to 50 minutes, or until the edges are browned, and the center is set. Warm the remaining 1 teaspoon honey with the orange juice. Brush this onto the warm cake—it'll sink right in—then let it cool completely in the pan. To serve, garnish slices with whipped cream, chopped almonds or pistachios, and a dusting of powdered sugar.

Nutrition:

Calories: 219, Fat: 5.8g, Fiber: 6.4, Carbs: 32.1g, Protein: 3.2g

CHOCOLATE-COVERED PRETZELS

Time: 30 minutes - **Serving Size:** Yields as many chocolate-covered pretzels as there are in a bag - **Prep Time:** 10 minutes - **Cook Time:** 20 minutes

INGREDIENTS:

- 1 bag of pretzels
- 3 tablespoons powdered sugar
- ¼ cup cannabis butter

- 3 tablespoons cocoa powder

Equipment:

- Double boiler
- Baking sheet
- Wax paper

DIRECTIONS:

1. Using the double boiler, melt the cannabutter.
2. When the cannabis butter is completely melted, use a sieve to add the powdered sugar and cocoa powder. A sieve will get rid of clumps and aerate the dry ingredients.
3. Over low heat, stir the mixture until all the ingredients have been well incorporated and a smooth texture is achieved.
4. Once smooth and combined, switch off the heat but leave the double boiler on the stovetop.
5. Line a baking sheet with wax paper and set it down next to the stove.
6. Using a fork, add the pretzels to the chocolate sauce mixture one at a time, dipping them in and removing them with the fork. Shake each pretzel lightly to remove excess chocolate sauce.
7. Place the pretzels on the lined baking sheet as you finish coating each one.
8. Place the baking sheet in the fridge and chill the pretzels until set.
9. Store in an airtight container.

S'MORES CANNABIS BROWNIES

Time: 45 minutes - **Serving Size:** 10 s'mores brownie squares - **Prep Time:** 10 minutes - **Cook Time:** 35 minutes

INGREDIENTS:

- ¼ cup of cannabis butter, melted
- ¼ cup of either sunflower oil or a light vegetable oil
- 1 cup brown sugar
- 1 teaspoon vanilla extract
- ½ cup all-purpose flour or whole wheat flour
- ¼ teaspoon sea salt
- 1/3 teaspoon baking powder
- 1/3 cup unsweetened cocoa powder
- 1 cup miniature marshmallows
- 4 graham crackers
- 8 ounces of milk chocolate

Equipment:

* Deep medium-sized baking pan or dish
* Parchment paper
* Large mixing bowl
* Whisk

DIRECTIONS:

1. Set the heat of your oven to 350° F and let it heat up while you prepare the brownies.
2. Line a deep medium-sized baking dish with a piece of parchment paper.
3. Whisk the eggs, sea salt, vanilla extract, brown sugar, and baking powder in a mixing bowl until the ingredients are well incorporated.
4. Add the flour and cocoa powder and mix again.
5. Add the melted cannabis butter and sunflower or light vegetable oil.
6. Pour the brownie mixture into the prepared baking dish or pan.
7. Place the dish in the oven and bake for approximately 15 minutes.
8. While you are waiting for the brownies to bake, crush the graham crackers and chop up the milk chocolate.
9. Add the broken-up graham crackers, miniature marshmallows, and milk chocolate to a mixing bowl.
10. Once the 15 minutes is up and the brownies are done baking, remove the baking dish from the oven and sprinkle the graham cracker, mini marshmallow, and chocolate mixture over the top.
11. Place the baking dish back into the oven and bake for another 15 to 20 minutes or until an inserted toothpick or skewer comes out clean.
12. Remove from the oven and place on a countertop to cool before cutting. Cut the baked brownie mix into 10 squares.

PEANUT BRITTLE

Time: 45 minutes - **Serving Size:** 10 servings of broken-up peanut brittle - **Prep Time:** 15 minutes - **Cook Time**: 30 minutes

INGREDIENTS:

* ½ a cup of cannabis sugar
* 1 tablespoon regular butter (cannabis butter may be substituted for a more potent peanut brittle, depending on your preference)
* ¼ teaspoon sea salt
* ½ a cup of peanuts, shelled

Equipment:

* Jelly roll pan
* Saucepan

- Parchment paper

DIRECTIONS:

1. Use parchment paper to line the jelly roll pan and then set it aside.
2. Place the saucepan over medium heat and add the butter, or cannabis butter if you are substituting. Melt the butter completely.
3. Add the sea salt and cannabis sugar to the melted butter and stir until the dry ingredients are entirely dissolved.
4. Once dissolved, remove the saucepan from the heat and add in the shelled peanuts. Mix well to evenly and thoroughly coat all the peanuts without too much clumping together.
5. Quickly pour the peanut brittle mixture into the lined jelly roll pan and use a spoon or spatula to spread the mixture into an even layer.
6. Place the pan into the fridge and chill for 30 minutes or until set and brittle.
7. Remove the brittle from the pan, peel off the parchment paper, being careful not to leave any paper behind in the brittle, and break up the brittle by smashing it with a rolling pin or other heavy object.
8. Divide the brittle up into 10 equal amounts, place each portion into a sealable bag and store.

MARSHMALLOWS

Time: 50 minutes plus cooling time - **Serving Size:** 18 servings - **Prep Time:** 20 minutes - **Cook Time:** 30 minutes

INGREDIENTS:

- 1 cup of confectioner's sugar
- 2 cups of cannabis sugar
- 1 tablespoon of light corn syrup
- 1 ¼ cups water
- 4 tablespoons gelatin, unflavored
- 2 egg whites
- 1 teaspoon vanilla extract

Equipment:

- 9-inch by 9-inch dish or pan
- Saucepans
- Bowls
- Candy thermometer
- Hand mixer or standing mixer

DIRECTIONS:

1. Generously dust your dish or pan with confectioner's sugar

2. Set your stovetop to medium-high heat and place a saucepan over the heat with the cannabis sugar, corn syrup, and ¾ cup of the water in it. Stir well and allow the mixture to heat up until it reaches a temperature of between 250° and 265° F. You can use a candy thermometer to check the temperature or, if you don't have one, you can check that the syrup is ready when a small dollop dropped into some cold water becomes a solid ball.

3. While the syrup is cooking, create a double boiler with a deep saucepan or small pot and a bowl that fits over it. Bring some water to a simmer in the saucepan or pot. Place the bowl over the simmering water, without it touching the water, with the remaining water from the recipe in it and sprinkle the gelatin on top of the water. Let the bowl sit over the simmering water until the gelatin has completely dissolved, then set it aside in a warm place until the syrup has reached the desired temperature.

4. Once the syrup mixture has reached the right temperature, add the gelatin mixture to it and whisk well. Set the syrup and gelatin aside again.

5. In another bowl, whisk the egg whites until they form soft peaks. A hand mixer or a stand mixer is ideal for this, as using a whisk requires a lot of arm power and stamina.

6. While continuing to beat the egg whites, start pouring the gelatin and syrup mixture into the whites. Pour slowly so that the syrup is poured in as a thin stream of liquid. The egg whites will become very stiff; this is when you add the vanilla extract.

7. Pour the marshmallow mix into the dish or pan that you prepared and let it set for around 8 hours before cutting into squares.

8. Store the balance in an airtight container in the fridge for an easy snack.

POP TARTS

Time: 45 minutes - **Serving Size**: 10 pop tarts - **Prep Time**: 20 minutes - **Cook Time**: 25 minutes

INGREDIENTS:

- 1 cup cannabis butter cut into cubes
- 2 cups all-purpose flour
- 1 tablespoon white sugar
- 1 teaspoon salt
- ¼ cup cold water
- ½ teaspoon vanilla extract
- 1 jar or package of your preferred frosting

Filling ingredients:

- ¼ cup softened cannabis butter
- 2 tablespoons ground cinnamon
- ¼ cup white sugar

Equipment:

* Baking sheets
* Parchment paper
* Mixing bowls
* Blunt knife
* Plastic wrap

DIRECTIONS:

1. Start by making the pop tarts themselves before the filling.
2. In a mixing bowl, add the salt, 1 tablespoon of the white sugar, and the flour. Mix the ingredients together.
3. Add the cannabis butter and cut it into the flour mix with a blunt knife. You can also use your fingers to rub the butter in. The mix will take on a crumb-like appearance and texture.
4. Mix in the vanilla extract and then add in the cold water slowly, one tablespoon at a time, mixing continuously. The dough will start sticking together until you can shape it into a ball.
5. Divide your dough into two equal quantities for better chilling and wrap each portion of dough in plastic wrap. Refrigerate the dough for at least an hour, if not longer.
6. While the dough is chilling, make the filling by whipping together all the filling ingredients in a mixing bowl. Set them aside until the dough has chilled.
7. Preheat your oven to 375° F.
8. While your oven is heating up, prepare your baking sheets by lining them with parchment paper and then setting them aside while you make the pop tarts.
9. Once sufficiently chilled, remove the dough from the fridge and roll it out flat on a floured surface. Roll the dough to a thickness of ½-inch.
10. Cut the rolled-out dough into 10 evenly sized rectangles.
11. Spoon a tablespoon of filling onto one half of each rectangle. Fold the other half of the rectangle over the filling and press down on the edges with a fork to seal the filling inside of the dough pocket.
12. Use the fork to poke holes in the top of each pop tart.
13. Place the tarts on the baking sheets and place them in the oven to bake for 25 minutes or until golden brown in color.
14. Remove the pop tarts from the oven and allow them to cool for around 15 minutes before frosting and enjoying.
15. Store the balance in an airtight container for an easy-to-grab snack.

RICE KRISPIE TREATS

Time: 20 minutes plus cooling time - **Serving Size:** Dependent on the size of the bars - **Prep Time:** 10 minutes - **Cook Time:** 10 minutes

INGREDIENTS:

- ½ cup cannabis butter
- 5 cups cereal (Rice Krispies, Cocoa Pebbles, Fruity Pebbles, etc.)
- 4 cups miniature marshmallows or regular marshmallows cut up

Equipment:

- Large saucepan
- 13-inch by 9-inch baking pan or dish
- Spatula or wooden spoon
- Non-stick cooking spray (optional) or butter for greasing

DIRECTIONS:

1. Grease your casserole dish with butter or non-stick cooking spray and set aside.
2. Place a large saucepan over medium to low heat and add in your cannabis butter. Allow the butter to melt completely but be careful not to let it burn.
3. Once the butter has melted, add in the miniature marshmallows and start stirring with that spatula or wooden spoon. Stir well as the marshmallows melt so that you evenly distribute the cannabis butter through the marshmallow mixture.
4. Once everything is melted, remove the saucepan from the heat and add in your cereal of choice. This is where the stirring becomes harder work, but it's important to mix all the ingredients thoroughly so that everything is evenly coated.
5. Once everything is well combined, spoon the cereal mix into the prepared pan or dish. Spread it out in an even layer and then compress it by pressing down firmly with your fingers. You may want to grease your hands with some butter before pressing down on the mixture to avoid it sticking to your hands.
6. Chill the cereal treats in the fridge or allow to set at room temperature until completely set before slicing into bars.
7. Store the balance in an airtight container.

CANDIED BACON

Time: 35 minutes - **Serving Size:** 12 pieces of cannabis candied bacon - **Prep Time**: 10 minutes - **Cook Time**: 25 minutes

INGREDIENTS:

- 12 slices of thick-cut bacon of your choice
- 1/3 cup of brown sugar
- 1 ½ teaspoons chili powder
- ¼ teaspoon cayenne pepper
- 1 gram of average decarbed cannabis, ground up

Equipment:

- Baking sheet
- Mixing bowl

DIRECTIONS:

1. Start with setting the temperature of your oven to 350° F and let it preheat while you prepare the bacon.
2. In a mixing bowl, combine the ground cannabis, brown sugar, chili powder, and cayenne pepper and mix together well.
3. Evenly coat both sides of each slice of bacon with the cannabis-sugar mix before laying them on a baking sheet. Be sure to space the bacon slices evenly apart.
4. Sprinkle any leftover sugar mix over the top of the bacon.
5. Place the baking sheet in the center of your oven and bake for 25 minutes or until the bacon is caramelized and crisp. Flip the bacon pieces halfway through baking.
6. Store in an airtight container in the fridge for a day or so as an easy snack.

CHOCOLATE STRAWBERRIES

Time: 30 minutes plus cooling time - **Serving Size:** ½ lb. of chocolate covered strawberries - **Prep Time:** 10 minutes - **Cook Time**: 20 minutes

INGREDIENTS:

- 1 tablespoon cannabis olive oil
- ½ lb. fresh strawberries with their stems still attached
- 1/8 cup of white chocolate melting wafers
- 1 cup milk chocolate melting wafers

Equipment:

- Baking sheet
- Parchment paper
- Pot and mixing bowl to create a double boiler

DIRECTIONS:

1. Line a baking sheet with parchment paper and set it aside.
2. Rinse off the strawberries, checking for imperfections or bugs, and pat them dry with a kitchen towel. Ensure that they are completely dry and set them aside.
3. Pour water into your base pot for your double boiler, place the pot over medium heat, and bring the water to a simmer.
4. Once the water is simmering, place your mixing bowl over the water but not touching it, and add your milk chocolate melting wafers. Melt the chocolate completely, stirring as it melts. Once melted, remove the chocolate from the heat.

5. Add your cannabis olive oil to the chocolate and stir in thoroughly. Ensure an even distribution of the oil through the chocolate so that each strawberry has the same potency.

6. Place the chocolate, strawberries, and prepared baking sheet next to each other for easy coating.

7. Holding the strawberries by their stems, dip each one into the infused melted milk chocolate, covering almost the whole strawberry. As you remove the strawberry from the chocolate, allow the excess chocolate to drip off back into the bowl. Lay each strawberry on the baking sheet, spacing them evenly apart.

8. Set the strawberries aside to set while you prepare the white chocolate.

9. Using a separate bowl, return to your double boiler with the white chocolate melting wafers and repeat the melting process as with the milk chocolate.

10. Once the white chocolate is completely melted, carefully place the bowl next to the baking sheet of setting strawberries. Use a spoon to drizzle the white chocolate generously and creatively over the milk chocolate covering the strawberries.

11. Store the balance in the fridge in an airtight container.

CHEEBA CHOCOLATE CHIP COOKIES

Cook Time: 10 minutes

If you love nuts in your cookies, try adding them with the chocolate chips!

INGREDIENTS:

- ½ cup cannabutter, softened
- ½ cup real butter, softened
- 2 ¼ cups all-purpose flour
- 1 teaspoon baking soda
- ¾ cup brown sugar
- ¼ cup white sugar
- 2 eggs
- 1 teaspoon vanilla extract
- 2 cups semisweet chocolate chip s

DIRECTIONS:

1. Heat oven to 350 degrees F. Spray 2 cookie sheets with nonstick spray.

2. With an electric mixer, mix cannabutter, butter, brown sugar, white sugar, baking soda, eggs and vanilla until combined. Add flour, mix until combined. Add chocolate chips, mix until combined.

3. Roll the dough by hand into 1 inch balls, and evenly place cookies 2 inches apart from each other onto the cookie sheets.

4. Bake 10 minutes.

5. Serve warm.

PUMPKIN POT BROWNIES

INGREDIENTS:

- 2/3 cup packed brown sugar
- 1/2 cup canned pumpkin
- 1 whole egg
- 2 egg whites
- 1/4 cup cannabutter
- 1 cup all-purpose flour
- 1 teaspoon baking powder
- 1 teaspoon unsweetened cocoa powder
- 1/2 teaspoon ground cinnamon
- 1/2 teaspoon ground allspice
- 1/4 teaspoon salt
- 1/4 teaspoon ground nutme g
- 1/3 cup miniature semisweet chocolate pieces

DIRECTIONS:

1. Preheat oven to 350 degrees F.

2. In a large mixing bowl, combine brown sugar, pumpkin, the whole egg, egg whites and oil.

3. Beat with an electric mixer on medium speed until blended.

4. Add flour, baking powder, cocoa powder, cinnamon, allspice, salt and nutmeg.

5. Beat on low speed until smooth. Stir in semisweet chocolate pieces.

6. Spray an 11×7 inch baking pan with nonstick coating.

7. Pour batter into pan. Spread evenly.

8. Bake 15 to 20 minutes or until a toothpick inserted near the center comes out clean.

ROCKY ROAD MARIJUANA BROWNIES

INGREDIENTS:

- 1/2 cup cannabis-infused butter
- 1/8 cup butter
- 2 ounces unsweetened chocolate
- 4 ounces bittersweet or semisweet chocolate
- 3/4 cup all-purpose flou r

- 1/2 teaspoon salt
- 1 cup granulated sugar
- 2 large eggs
- 1 teaspoon vanilla extract
- 3/4 cup toasted almond slices
- 1 cup miniature marshmallows

DIRECTIONS:

1. Preheat the oven to 350 degrees F. Line an 8-inch square baking pan with aluminum foil, and grease foil with either butter or vegetable shortening.

2. marijuana brownies, lining the pan

3. Melt the cannabutter, butter and chocolates over low heat in a medium saucepan stirring frequently. Set aside to cool for 5 minutes.

4. Stir together the flour and salt; set aside.

5. Stir the sugar into the melted cannabutter until well combined.

6. Beat in the eggs and vanilla and continue mixing until well incorporated.

7. Mix in the flour and salt until just incorporated.

8. Reserve 1/2 cup of the brownie batter, and spread the remainder into the prepared pan.

9. Bake batter in the pan for about 20 minutes. While it is baking, prepare the topping by stirring together the reserved batter with the toasted almonds and marshmallows .

10. After batter in pan has baked for 20 minute, remove from oven.

11. Spread topping over par-baked brownies and return to oven. Bake for about 10 more minutes or until marshmallows are browned and a toothpick inserted in the center comes out with just a few moist crumbs clinging to it.

12. Let cool in pan before using the foil to lift out the brownies and slice.

HONEY CHOCOLATE BROWNIES

INGREDIENTS:

- 1 cup melted marijuana butter or oil
- ½ cup melted unsweetened chocolate or cocoa powder
- 4 eggs
- 1 cup honey
- 2 teaspoons vanilla
- 2 cups unbleached white flour
- 2 teaspoons baking powder
- ½ teaspoon sea salt

- 1 cup raisin s
- 1 cup chopped nuts

DIRECTIONS:

1. Preheat oven to 350 degrees F.

2. Whip the butter, chocolate, carob or cocoa and honey together until smooth. Add eggs and vanilla; mix well.

3. Add the dry ingredients, stir until dampened. Add the raisins and nuts and mix thoroughly.

4. Pour batter into a greased 9x13 inch baking pan. Bake for 45 minutes or until done.

5. Cut into 24 equal pieces (approximately 2" x 2"), each serving has 2 teaspoons of butter = high dose, or cut into 48 pieces (about 2" x 1") = medium dose.

MICROWAVE PEANUT BUTTER SWIRL BROWNIE

INGREDIENTS:

- 2 tablespoons cannabutter, softened
- 2 tablespoons sugar
- 1 1/2 tablespoons brown sugar
- 1 tablespoon cocoa powder
- 1 egg yolk
- 3 tablespoons flour
- Pinch of salt
- Splash of vanilla
- 1 tablespoon creamy peanut butter

DIRECTIONS:

1. Mix the cannabutter, sugar, brown sugar, vanilla and egg yolk until smooth .

2. Stir in the salt and flour until well combined. Stir chocolate chips in last.

3. Pour into a ramekin or mug, then dot the top with peanut butter.

4. Swirl lightly with a butter knife.

5. Microwave for 45-75 seconds in the microwave until just done.

CANNACRACK

Prep Time: 5 minutes - **Cook Time**: 15 minutes

INGREDIENTS:

- 1/3 cup cannabutter
- 9 cups Chex cereal
- 1 cup semisweet chocolate chip s
- ½ cup peanut butter
- 1 teaspoon vanilla extract
- 1 ½ cups powdered sugar

DIRECTIONS:

1. Place the cereal into a 1 gallon Ziplock freezer bag.

2. In a saucepan and on medium heat, add everything except the powdered sugar. Stir until melted and combined.

3. Pour the chocolate mixture onto the cereal inside the Ziplock bag. Seal the bag and shake it until all the cereal is coated with the chocolate mixture. Once the cereal is coated, pour the powdered sugar into the Ziplock bag, seal it, and shake it until the powdered sugar has coated everything.

4. Let cool, store in the same Ziplock bag, and eat with caution.

OVEN-BAKED DONUT HOLES

Time Required: 50 minutes

These donuts can be filled with your favorite pudding, jelly or sweet cream.

INGREDIENTS:

- 1 cup white sugar
- ½ cup cannabutter, melted
- ¾ teaspoon ground nutmeg
- ½ cup milk
- 1 teaspoon baking powder
- 1 cup all purpose flour
- 1 teaspoon ground cinnamon

DIRECTIONS :

1. Heat oven to 350 degrees F. Spray all of the cups of a mini-muffin pan with nonstick cooking spray.

2. With an electric stand mixer, mix ½ cup sugar, nutmeg, ¼ cup cannabutter, milk, baking powder and flour until combined

3. Fill mini-muffin cups ½ way full with donut mix. Bake 20 minutes.

4. When donuts are in oven, take 2 separate bowls and put ¼ cup melted cannabutter in one, and ½ cup sugar with cinnamon in the other.

5. When donuts have finished baking, remove them from the mini-muffin pan and, one-at-a-time, dip them first in the melted cannabutter followed by coating them with the cinnamon sugar.

6. Let cool.

BAKED BACKLAVA

INGREDIENTS:

- 1 1/2 pounds walnuts, chopped
- 2 cups sugar
- 1/2 teaspoon nutmeg
- 3 teaspoons cinnamon
- 3 sticks canna butter
- 16 ounces phyllo dough
- 1 1/2 cups water
- 1 1/2 teaspoons Lemon Juic e
- 2 cups honey
- 1/2 teaspoon vanilla

DIRECTIONS:

1. Preheat oven to 300 degrees F.

2. Set aside 2 tablespoons of the cannabutter. With the remaining butter, grease a 10×15 inch baking dish.

3. Take 10 sheets of phyllo dough, coat each with a good layer of butter and place them in the baking pan.

4. Mix together the walnuts with one cup of sugar, and pour this evenly into the pan over the phyllo dough sheets.

5. Take another five layers of phyllo dough, butter them and then place them in the pan as well. Bake the dough for 50 minutes.

6. While this is baking, take a saucepan and mix the leftover sugar with the spices, vanilla, water and lemon; cook until the mixture is syrupy. Add honey and heat for a minute. Remove from heat.

7. Cut the baklava into 2 by 2 inch squares or any other shape you want and then pour the syrup over them.

8. Now, have patience- set aside for two days so as to allow the honey to permeate. You are now ready for this spicy canna treat.

BUTTERSCOTCH CANNA-POPS

INGREDIENTS:

- 1 cup sugar
- ½ cup cannabis corn syrup
- 2 tablespoons water
- 1 ½ teaspoons vinegar

- ¼ cup cannabutte r
- ¼ teaspoon vanilla extract
- Lollipop sticks

DIRECTIONS:

1. Line baking sheet with waxed paper; set aside. Use cannabutter to grease the sides of the saucepan.

2. Combine the sugar, cannabis corn syrup, water and vinegar. Cook over medium-high heat for about 5 minutes to boiling, stirring constantly with a wooden spoon to dissolve the sugar. Continue to cook the mixture over medium heat, stirring constantly, while adding the butter (cut into 8 pieces), 2 pieces at a time.

3. The candy mixture should boil at a moderate, steady rate over the entire surface. Wait for a candy thermometer to read 300 degrees. This should take 25 to 30 minutes.

4. Remove the saucepan from the heat. Stir in the vanilla extract. Cool for 5 minutes.

5. Pour the mixture, 1 to 2 tablespoons at a time, onto the lined baking sheets. The mixture will make 2 to 3 inch circles.

6. Quickly place a lollipop stick into each piece of candy, twisting gently to cover with the candy mixture. Let the lollipops harden. Wrap the lollipops individually in clear plastic wrap to store at room temperature.

CANNABIS HARD CANDY

INGREDIENTS:

- 1 cup cannabutter
- 2 cups white sugar
- ¾ cup water
- ¼ cup honey
- ½ cup corn or rice syrup
- ½ teaspoon sea salt
- 1 teaspoon vanilla or almond extract
- 2 tablespoons regular butter or coconut oi l

DIRECTIONS:

1. Heat your honey and cannabutter to the point that they're in a liquid, pourable state. Set aside.

2. Use the regular butter or coconut oil to coat your candy molds.

3. Heat sugar, water and corn/rice syrup in a saucepan. Cover without stirring and bring to a boil.

4. Once the mixture is boiling, use a candy thermometer to check heat until the temperature reaches 132°C, the "soft-crack" stage. This should take about 15 minutes past the point of boiling.

5. Stir in cannabutter, salt and honey and continue heating until the mixture reaches 148°C. This is the "hard-crack" stage, and now the mixture should bubble to the edges of the pot.

6. Turn off the heat, wait for the bubbles to subside, and stir in the vanilla or almond extract.

7. Pour the mixture into the molds. If you're using lollipop sticks, place one end in the mold with the candy.

8. Allow the candy to cool for 30–60 minutes. Press the candy out of the molds afterwards.

9. Wrap the candy in aluminum foil or wax paper and refrigerate .

PINA CO-CANNA PIE CAKE

INGREDIENTS:

- 1½ cups Graham crackers, crumbled
- ½ cup cannabutter, softened
- 16 ounces (2- 8 ounce packages) cream cheese, softened
- ½ cup cream of coconut
- ½ cup Cool Whip
- ½ cup pineapple, crushed diced
- ½ cup cherries, dice d
- 1 cup coconut, shredded

DIRECTIONS:

1. Mix graham cracker crumbs and softened cannabutter in a large bowl.

2. Transfer crust mixture to 9x13 inch baking pan. Press down firmly to cover surface of baking pan with Graham cracker mixture.

3. Beat cream cheese and cream of coconut together until smooth.

4. Add cool whip, pineapple and cherries. Fold ingredients together until evenly mixed.

5. Spread filling mixture on top of the Graham cracker crust. Top with shredded coconut.

6. Chill cake in refrigerator for 2 hours. Serve and enjoy.

RED-HOT WHITE FUDGE

INGREDIENTS:

- 1 (14 oz) can sweetened condensed milk
- 12 ounce bag of white chocolate chips
- 2-4 ounce baking bars Ghirardelli white chocolate
- 2 jars red hot cinnamon candies (i.e. Red Hots or Cake Mate cinnamon decors)
- 12-14 drops cinnamon flavoring oil
- 2 tablespoons cannabis-infused coconut oil (melted)

DIRECTIONS:

1. Line an 8×8 inch pan with wax paper, making sure that the wax paper covers all the way up the sides of the pan.

2. Pour the sweetened condensed milk into a medium-size sauce pan.

3. Grab the white chocolate chips and break up the white chocolate bars; add them both to the condensed milk in your sauce pan.

4. Place the sauce pan over medium-low heat on your stove top, and melt the 3 ingredients together until the chocolate and milk are smooth.

5. Once the ingredients are creamy and smooth, add the 2 tablespoons of cannabis-infused coconut oil, and mix until the oil is fully combined with the chocolate. (The coconut oil will add a nice sheen to the fudge, too!)

6. After the coconut oil is combined, remove the sauce pan from the heat.

7. Stir in the 12-14 drops of cinnamon oil, tasting the chocolate afterwards and adjusting if you desire more spice. (Keep in mind you will also be adding the cinnamon candies) .

8. Add 1½ bottles of your cinnamon candies. (You will be using the remaining ½ bottle of candies to decorate the tops of your white fudge.)

9. Once the candies are mixed in, pour the white fudge batter into your prepped baking dish, spreading the fudge out with a spatula to ensure a smooth top and filled-in corners.

10. Place the remaining cinnamon candies on top of the fudge while trying to keep in mind how you will be slicing up the fudge. (I recommend standard rectangle pieces.)

11. Place the white fudge into the refrigerator, and chill the fudge for at least 2-3 hours or until firm.

12. Remove the white fudge from th e refrigerator, and carefully lift the sides of the wax paper to remove it from the pan. Carefully remove the wax paper from the fudge itself.

13. If you are giving the fudge as a gift, I suggest you cut off the edge pieces, as they will appear to be a little wrinkled in appearance. Nonetheless, they are still delicious!

14. Proceed to cut the cinnamon white fudge into pieces that fit your liking.

15. Serve immediately and enjoy! You can store the fudge pieces in the refrigerator for up to one week.

CANNABIS HARD CANDY AND LOLLIPOP

INGREDIENTS:

- 1 cup sugar
- 1/3 cup corn syrup
- 1/2 cup water
- 1/4 teaspoon cream of tartar
- 1/4 to 1 teaspoon flavoring
- Liquid food coloring
- 1 to 2 teaspoon(s) citric acid (optional)
- 3 tablespoons cannabis tinctur e

DIRECTIONS:

1. Prepare either a marble slab or an upside-down cookie sheet (air underneath the sheet will help the candy to cool faster) by covering it with parchment paper and spraying it with oil. If you're using molds, prepare the molds with lollipop sticks, spray with oil, and place them on a cookie sheet or marble slab.

2. In your pan, over medium heat, stir together the sugar, corn syrup, water and cream of tartar with a wooden spoon until the sugar crystals dissolve.

3. Continue to stir, using a pastry brush dampened with warm water to dissolve any sugar crystals clinging to the sides of the pan, then stop stirring as soon as the syrup starts to boil.

4. Place the candy thermometer in the pan, being careful not to let it touch the bottom or sides, and let the syrup boil without stirring until the thermometer just reaches 300 degrees F (hard-crack stage).

5. Remove the pan from the heat immediately, and let the syrup cool to about 275 degrees F before adding flavor, color, cannabis tincture and citric acid (adding it sooner causes most of the flavor to cook away) .

6. Be careful! The sugar syrup is extremely hot! If you burn yourself, run cold water over your hand for several minutes, but do not apply ice.

7. Working quickly, pour the syrup into the prepared molds and let cool for about 10 minutes. If you're not using molds, pour small (2-inch) circles onto the prepared marble slab or cookie sheet, and place a lollipop stick in each one, twisting the stick to be sure it's covered with candy.

8. Let the lollipops cool for at least 10 minutes, until they are hard. Wrap individually in plastic wrap or cellophane and seal with tape or twist ties.

9. Store in a cool, dry place.

CANNABIS TOFFEE CANDY

INGREDIENTS:

- 2 cups roasted nuts (I like pecans)
- 1 cup sugar
- 1 cup butter (or cannabutter)
- 1 tablespoon light corn syrup
- 1/4 cup water
- 1 cup chocolate morsels

Directions:

1. Spread about 1 1/2 cups of chopped nuts on a non-stick baking sheet (may need to lightly grease it, but not too much) .

2. Bring sugar, butter and corn syrup to a boil over medium heat, stirring constantly to prevent burning.

3. Cook until the mixture reads about 300 to 310 degrees and mixture is golden brown (use candy thermometer and work fast; once it reaches 300, there isn't a lot of time until it burns).

4. Pour sugar mixture over chopped nuts on the baking sheet. Spread chocolate over hot candy and spread with a spoon (chocolate will start melting as soon as it hits the candy).

5. Sprinkle the rest of the nuts over the top of the chocolate, and let the sheet cool for about 30 mins or until the candy is cool.

6. The candy should break apart pretty easily after it has cooled.

CANNABIS PEANUT BUTTER BALLS

Items Needed:

- Mixing bowl
- Double boiler
- Tray
- Wax paper
- Toothpicks

INGREDIENTS:

- 1 1/2 cups peanut butter
- 1 cup cannabutter (hardened)
- 4 cups confectioners' suga r
- 1 1/3 cups Graham cracker crumbs
- 2 cups semisweet chocolate chips
- 1 tablespoon shortening

DIRECTIONS:

1. Place the peanut butter and the cannabutter in a large mixing bowl. Slowly blend in the confectioners' sugar making sure that it does not get messy. Add Graham cracker crumbs and mix till consistency becomes solid enough to shape into balls. Make one-inch diameter balls.

2. Melt the chocolate chips and shortening in a double bottomed boiler. Prick a toothpick into each ball, and then dip them one by one in the chocolate mixture. Place the chocolate wrapped balls on wax paper on a tray. Place in the freezer for about 30 minutes until the balls are all solid.

3. This is an easy way to have a sweet snack and a cannabis kick at the same time. Just don't gobble them all down at once; go gradually, savor them, and relish them like you really want to. Share these awesome peanut butter balls with your friends, so that you all can feel the mellow kick coming on slowly, sweetly but surely!

RICE KRISPIE TREATS

INGREDIENTS:

- 1 bag miniature marshmallows (use fruit flavored marshmallows to change it up)

- 2 tablespoons unsalted butter (cannabis-infused butter)
- 2 tablespoons coconut oil (cannabis-infused coconut oil)
- 5 cups crispy rice cereal
- ¼ teaspoon almond extract (try a raspberry or strawberry with fruit flavored marshmallows)
- Note: You can choose to use both infused butter and coconut oil or just use one or the other.

DIRECTIONS:

1. Spray bottom of cookie sheet with cooking spray (or parchment paper makes easier cleanup).

2. In pan over medium heat, melt butter, infused oil and extract together.

3. Continue heating over medium heat, and slowly add marshmallows to the mixture, stirring constantly to prevent scorching.

4. When the mixture is well-blended (remember don't overcook), remove from heat and immediately add cereal in small portions until the cereal is evenly covered. (Tip: Coat your spoon with a little oil first.)

5. Spread out onto cookie sheet, and press down with spoon into desired thickness.

6. Allow to cool and then cut into individual portions (15-20 servings).

7. Chocolate lovers can drizzle canna-shell chocolate across the top before cooling.

Caution

1. Too Much Caffeine Can Negatively Affect Your Experience:

2. If using chocolate in your recipe, please consider that caffeine is found naturally in cocoa beans, so any chocolate has a little bit of the stimulant. Candy bars generally have less than 10 milligrams, but the darker the chocolate, the higher the caffeine content.

CANNABIS APPLE PIE

Time Required: 2 Hours

INGREDIENTS:

- 9-inch pie dish
- 2 sheets of refrigerated pie crusts
- 6 cups apples, cored, peeled, and sliced (Granny Smith, Golden Delicious, and/or HoneyCrisp)
- 1 tablespoon fresh lemon juice
- ⅓ cup brown sugar
- ½ cup granulated sugar
- ⅛ cup flour
- 1 teaspoon cinnamon, ground
- ½ teaspoon salt
- ⅛ teaspoon nutmeg, ground
- 1½ cups cannabutter, cube d

DIRECTIONS :

1. Preheat oven to 375 degrees.

2. Press one pie crust sheet firmly into the bottom of the pie dish and up the sides of the pan.

3. Trim the edge of the dough with kitchen scissors; leave 1 inch of dough to hang over the edge of pan. Set aside.

4. Combine the apples and lemon juice in a large bowl. Mix well.

5. Add brown sugar, granulated sugar, flour, cinnamon, salt and nutmeg.

6. Mix well, making sure to coat all the apples.

7. Transfer the filling mix to the dough-lined pan.

8. Disperse cubed cannabutter on top of the apple filling evenly.

9. Place the second pie sheet over the filled pie. Trim edges appropriately, leaving 1 inch of dough hanging.

10. Fold the edge of the top layer of dough under the edge of the bottom layer of dough. Pinch dough sheets together to seal.

11. Cut an "x" across the top center of the dough to allow steam to escape.

12. Put the uncooked pie in the refrigerator to firm the dough (about 20 minutes).

13. Remove pie from refrigerator and bake the pie in the preheated oven for 1 hour, or until the crust is golden brown and the filling is bubbling.

14. Transfer pie to a wire rack and let cool to completely set for at least 1 hour before serving.

15. Serve with whipped canna-cream or cannabis ice cream for a heightened experience!

CANNABIS-INFUSED RED VELVET CAKE

INGREDIENTS:

- 2 3/4 cups all purpose flour
- 1 3/4 cups sugar
- 1 teaspoon baking soda
- 2 teaspoons cocoa powder
- 2 large eggs, room temperature
- ¾ cannabis oil (coconut, canola…)
- ¾ cup canola oil
- 1 1/4 cup buttermilk
- 2 teaspoons red food colorin g
- 1 teaspoon vanilla
- 1 tablespoon white vinegar
  For Frosting:
- 16 ounces cream cheese

- 4 ounces cannabis butter, slightly softened
- 3 cups powdered sugar
- 2 teaspoons vanilla

DIRECTIONS:

1. This cake is so very good; you will love having it in your repertoire. When you eat a slice that is medicated, be sure to save another sliver for later. It's one of those foods that you eat when you are stoned and want to just sit there eating it for the rest of your life. Fortunately, that feeling will pass, as it would not be a very productive, though delicious, experience.

2. Preheat oven to 325 degrees F.

3. Place parchment on the bottom of three 8-inch pans.

4. Mix all dry ingredients together. Beat eggs slightly. Add all wet ingredients together. Mix wet into dry ingredients.

5. Pour into prepared pans. Bake for 30 to 35 minutes.

6. When done, remove from oven and wait 5 minutes; then, turn out on cooling rack s

For Icing:

1. Place the butter in mixer and beat till soft. Add cream cheese and mix, stopping periodically to scrape bowl.

2. Beat till light colored; slowly add powdered sugar, waiting for it to be completely incorporated along with some air before adding more.

3. When all the sugar is incorporated, beat a few more minutes; add vanilla, beat and ice cake immediately.